CW00409309

2   A STUDY OF 3 ETHICAL THEORIES

Published independently by Tinderspark Press
© Jonathan Rowe 2019
www.philosophydungeon.weebly.com

CONTENTS

ABOUT THIS BOOK

This book offers advice for teachers and students approaching Edexcel AS or A-Level Religious Studies, Paper 2 (Religion & Ethics). It concentrates on **Topic 2 (A Study of 3 Ethical Theories)**. The other topics are:

1 **Significant Concepts in Issues/Debates in Religion & Ethics**

3 **Application of Ethical Theories to Issues of Importance**

The **Ethics AS/Year 1 Study Guide** will bring all 3 of these books together in one volume. These three study guides will be summarised in note format in **Revision Guide 1**, which will also include revision exercises, quizzes and exam-style questions for AS and A-Level but not have the sort of detailed explanations that are in the study guides.

Together with this one, these books will cover the AS course or Year 1 of the A-Level; the remaining books will cover the topics in Year 2 of the A-Level.

4 **Ethical Language**

5 **Deontology, Virtue Ethics & the Works of Scholars**

6 **Medical Ethics: beginning & end of life issues**

The **Ethics Year 2 Study Guide** will bring all 3 of these books together in one volume. These three study guides will be summarised in note format in **Revision Guide 2**, but there will also be **Revision Guide 3** covering all 6 study guides in note format and having exam questions for the entire A-Level (but not AS).

> Text that is indented and shaded like this is a quotation from a scholar or from the Bible. Candidates should use some of these quotations in their exam responses.

Text in this typeface and boxed represents the author's comments, observations and reflections. Such texts are not intended to guide candidates in writing exam answers.

Study guides are also available **for Topic 3 (New Testament Studies)** and **Topic 1 (Philosophy & Religion)** is supported on the **www.philosophydungeon.weebly.com** website

TOPIC 2: A STUDY OF 3 ETHICAL THEORIES

What's this topic about?

What are the main debates on contemporary ethics? How do religious ideas contribute to these debates and what arguments have been advanced from secular (non-religious) perspectives? This Topic focuses on two main areas:

2.1 UTILITARIANISM

This topic looks at the concept of **utility** and its influences, especially in the work of **Bentham** and **Mill**. Different types of Utilitarianism (**act, rule, preference, negative, ideal**) are examined. Students consider **strengths and weaknesses** of these positions as well as reforms to the **law** and **social attitudes**.

2.2 SITUATION ETHICS

This topic looks at the concept of **'new morality'** in the 20th century, the importance of **agape** (love) and the teachings of Jesus as well as the work of **Fletcher** and **Robinson**. Students consider **strengths and weaknesses** of these positions as well as changes to the **law** and **social attitudes**. **Anthology extract 1** relates to this topic.

2.3 NATURAL MORAL LAW

This topic looks at the concept of **telos** (purpose) in Biblical and classical ethics of **equality**, focusing on the **primary** and **secondary precepts** and **proportionalism**, as well as the work of **Aquinas** and **Hoose**. Students consider **strengths and weaknesses** of these positions as well as changes to the **law** and **social attitudes**.

Before you go any further...

... there are some things you need to know.

WHAT ARE DEONTOLOGICAL ETHICS?

DEONTOLOGY means 'duty-based'. Deontology is an approach in analytical ethics (or meta-ethics) that explains why some things are right or wrong by referring to **duties**.

Duties are things that a good person *must* do – or else things they *must never* do. For example, you might have a duty to be kind, keep your promises and respect your parents – or a duty not to lie, steal or commit murder.

Another way of understanding deontological ethics is that **the moral character of a behaviour is found in the act itself**. For example, lying is wrong because it involves dishonesty – not because it hurts people's feelings, disrupts society or makes you into an untrustworthy person. Of course, lying might *also* have these various bad consequences, but they are irrelevant for purposes of working out why lying is bad. Lying would still be bad if it had no bad consequence – or if it had good consequences!

If you are studying the full A-Level, you will study deontology in more depth in Topic 5.

Legalism & Absolutism

There are objections to a deontological view of ethics. One is LEGALISM, which is treating duties like a set of laws. The problem with this is that fulfill your duties **to the letter** and no more. For example, if you have a duty to give to charity, you might give the minimum possible amount: in a legalistic sense, you have 'done the right thing' but many people believe morality should be more than doing the bare minimum.

ABSOLUTISM is the idea that duties can never be questioned or altered: you have to obey them all the time. This produces problems when doing your duty produces misery or destruction. For example, being honest can lead to hurt feelings and betrayed secrets – or else keeping your promise can force you to take part in something criminal or cruel.

Conflicting Duties

A final problem is that duties can CONFLICT with each other. The classic example is the duty to be honest and the duty to keep a promise. What do you do when you promise to keep a secret but then someone asks you to tell the truth about it? For example, you promise to keep a secret about your friend's surprise birthday party, but then your friend asks if you have any plans on her birthday. Do you keep the promise (and lie) or tell the truth (and break the promise)?

WHAT ARE CONSEQUENTIALIST ETHICS?

The term CONSEQUENTIALISM was coined by **G.E. Anscombe (1958)** to describe ethical theories opposed to deontology. These theories **locate the moral character of behaviour in the consequences of that behaviour**. In other words, it's the consequences that determine whether an act is right or wrong.

For example, there is nothing wrong with lying. However, lying often makes people unhappy, which is bad; moreover, lying erodes trust in society. Put simply, lying tends to have bad consequences and these consequences are what make lying wrong. However, you can imagine many situations where lying does **not** lead to bad consequences – there are 'white lies' that protect people's feelings. If the consequences are good, then lying is good.

---

*Consequentialist ethics are sometimes called TELEOLOGICAL ethics, from the Greek 'telos' meaning "end". However, teleology is a word used in other parts of the Religious Studies course - notable in the **Design Argument for the Existence of God** in **Unit 1** - so I shall avoid using it here and stick to 'consequentialist' instead.*

Antinomianism & Relativism

ANTINOMIAN means 'against all laws' and is the opposite of legalism. This is the view that there are no hard-and-fast ethical rules and we can decide everything on a case-by-case basis. Many critics feel this would lead to chaos in society.

RELATIVISM is the view that there is no ultimate or absolute right and wrong: anything can be justified in certain situations. This means that, even though cannibalism, torture and child abuse are almost always wrong, in extreme circumstances they could be the right courses of action.

Many critics of consequentialism argue that these two viewpoints are highly undesirable. Antinomianism can lead to a complete breakdown of trust and security in society, since no one will be living by shared ethical rules. Relativism means that there are no human rights or unacceptable behaviours: people will try to justify even monstrous acts like genocide.

THE TROLLEY PROBLEM

This is a moral dilemma proposed by **Philippa Foot** in order to show different ethical theories in their clearest light. The Trolley Problem invites the reader to imagine that:

> *he is the driver of a runaway tram [trolley] which he can only steer from one narrow track on to another; five men are working on one track and one man on the other; anyone on the track the tram enters is bound to be killed* – **Philippa Foot (1967)**

> *Foot was British and refers to a runaway 'tram' but the problem was made famous a few years later by the American philosopher **Judith Thompson**, who substituted the US term 'trolley'. Modern examples often substitute a runaway train, but the problem has become known as 'the Trolley Problem' whatever vehicle is involved.*

Readers have to decide whether, as the driver of the runaway machine (or, in Thompson's version, a bystander at the junction), they would pull a lever to divert the tram/trolley onto a side-track, killing a single worker, or allow it to continue on the main track, killing five workers.

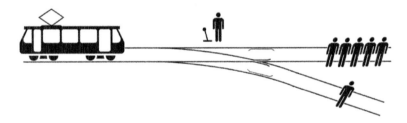

For a consequentialist, the best course of action is clear: pulling the lever results in fewer deaths so this is the ethical action. This is the popular solution for most people.

For a deontologist, things are less clear. Deontologists have a duty not to kill and pulling the lever is a decision to kill the solitary worker on the track. Allowing the tram/trolley to continue on its course will result in five deaths but, from a deontological viewpoint, that won't be anyone's fault, since it was unintentional.

Judith Thompson introduces a second version of the Trolley Problem, which proposes a bystander ('George') watching the approaching tram/trolley from a bridge:

> *The only way to stop an out-of-control trolley is to drop a very heavy weight into its path. But the only available, sufficiently heavy weight is a fat man, also watching the trolley from the footbridge. George can shove the fat man onto the track in the path of the trolley, killing the fat man; or he can refrain from doing this, letting the five die* – **Judith Thompson (1976)**

Thompson's 'fat man' variation makes clear the sacrifice involved: you are deliberately causing the death of one person in order to avoid the accidental deaths of five. Many consequentialists who would cheerfully pull the lever in Foot's version are reluctant to push the fat man off the bridge in Thompson's version. Yet the two courses of action seem to be, ethically, the same. For most readers, the deontological solution is now the popular one.

EVALUATING DEONTOLOGY & CONSEQUENTIALISM

You will be expected to evaluate the three ethical theories in this book and this usually boils down to locating them on the spectrum between deontology and consequentialism.

Deontology is the traditional way of looking at ethics. Most parents raise their children with fixed lists of 'dos' and 'don'ts' and this sort of ethical thinking is promoted at school, where school rules are often enforced in an inflexible way. Children often learn to complain *"it's not fair!"* when they are punished for something they didn't intend or didn't understand, or when they see other children getting away with something they are being punished for, or when the punishment seems out of proportion to what they did wrong – all of which might be their first insight into the weaknesses of deontology.

Many religions promote deontological ethics. Judaism and Christianity teach the TEN COMMANDMENTS (**Exodus 20: 1-17**) as a summation of all moral rules. Islam similarly offers rules for living which many believers regard as non-negotiable. However, all religions face the problem of people who follow the *letter* of these laws but ignore the *spirit* – for example, worshippers who keep all the rules and follow all the restrictions, but are still mean-spirited, big-headed or self-centred. Most of Jesus' teachings confront the problem of HYPOCRISY, which is people who are dutiful on the outside but who harbour evil thoughts:

> *On the outside you appear to people as righteous but on the inside you are full of hypocrisy and wickedness* – **Matthew 23: 28**

Typically, religious fundamentalists persist with a deontological view of ethics, but religious liberals reject **absolutism** and **legalism**. However, many of them feel just as uncomfortable with **antinomianism** and **relativism**. Later in this book, you will learn about **Situation Ethics** (p31) which tries to find a 'third way' between deontology and consequentialism.

Consequentialism is usually associated with secular ethics. Although it appears in the ethical ideas of **Aristotle**, it was championed by the atheist philosophers of the Enlightenment in 18th century Europe, notably **Jeremy Bentham** (p17, 77) and, later, **John Stuart Mill** (p15, 80).

The appeal of consequentialism is that it does not rely on religious Scriptures to reveal right and wrong or on religious leaders to interpret morality. Each rational human being can work out the consequences of their own actions and decide what is best. The Enlightenment also saw the rise of democratic governments and these politicians found in consequentialism an ethical theory ideally suited to working out what was for 'the common good' or would benefit the majority.

Not all Enlightenment thinkers embraced consequentialism. **Immanuel Kant (1724-1804)** revived deontology, but based it on human reason and without its old associations with religion and revelation.

TOPIC 2.1 UTILITARIANISM

Utilitarianism is a **consequentialist** (p7) theory of ethics that **locates the moral quality of an act in its consequences**. In other words, it is the consequences of an act that tells us whether the act is right or wrong. The best actions produce consequences that benefit the most people (or creatures) involved. Deciding on the right course of action is a matter of weighing up the likely consequences.

For a utilitarian, every action produces different amounts of UTILITY (usefulness, benefit, positive outcomes). This means there is never a 'good' thing to do or a 'bad' thing to do – but there is always a 'best' thing to do (the action that produces the *most* utility) and a 'worst' thing to do (producing the least *utility* – or **disutility**).

But what exactly is UTILITY?

What is Utility?

'Utility' just means 'value' or 'usefulness' but that is a rather vague definition. Most discussions of Utilitarianism turn into discussions of what 'utility' means: it is the fundamental moral outcome for utilitarians, the thing that makes everything else right or wrong, so it is important that they define it clearly.

Pleasure

Early utilitarians like **Jeremy Bentham** (p14, 77) defined utility as PLEASURE. This means that pleasure is what gives moral value to things: pleasurable things are good and painful things are bad.

> *Nature has placed mankind under the governance of two sovereign masters, pain and pleasure* – **Jeremy Bentham (1776)**

Notice Bentham says 'Nature' - not 'God' - is responsible for our attraction to pleasure and aversion to pain. Bentham's ideas are thoroughly secular and scientific.

If utility is understood as pleasure, then a utilitarian aims to maximize pleasure: the best actions produce the most pleasure for the most creatures capable of feeling pleasure; the worst actions produce pain rather than pleasure.

An important related idea is INSTRUMENTAL GOODS. These are things that do not produce pleasure (or reduce pain) in themselves, but are instrumental (useful) for making life more pleasurable or pain-free. For example, brushing your teeth isn't pleasurable, but it is instrumental for preventing tooth decay, which is very painful. This gives tooth brushing (and flossing, don't forget to floss!) high utility.

There are many things that humans value besides pleasure, such as honesty or education or courage. However, utilitarians can respond that these things are instrumental goods: by being honest, educated and brave, you are more likely to have a pleasant (or less painful) life.

Hedonism

Hedonism is the idea that pleasure is the point or purpose of a good life (from the Greek *hedone* meaning pleasure or delight). Hedonism in popular language means living your life for your *own* pleasure, normally through sex, drugs and laziness. However, the philosophical idea of HEDONISM is that the total amount of pleasure should be maximized: this includes everybody else's pleasure, not just your own.

This can be expressed by saying that ***the identity of the person experiencing pleasure or pain is not ethically significant***: someone else's pleasure counts for just as much as yours.

For example, spending your life taking drugs and playing video games might maximize your own pleasure but it would upset your parents, frustrate your teachers and probably annoy your friends too. Their displeasure more than outweighs your pleasure, so according to hedonism it would be wrong for you to live this way.

Henry Sidgwick compares **universalistic hedonism** (trying to make society happier, even at the cost of sacrificing yourself) with **psychological hedonism** (working towards your own happiness and the happiness of people you know and care about).

Bentham proposes that you can calculate overall pleasure through HEDONIC CALCULUS (also called **felicific calculus**):

1. Add up the total amount of pleasure an action might produce for everyone concerned (measured in '**hedons**')
2. Deduct the total amount of pain the action might produce for everyone concerned (measured in '**dolors**')
3. The action which produces the highest total is ethically right

> *Bentham doesn't actually tell us how much pleasure makes up one hedon or how much pain makes up one dolor. In fact, judging pleasure/pain is very subjective, which points towards a problem with hedonic calculus. If drinking a glass of wine gives me pleasure tonight but a headache tomorrow, is the headache's pain more or less than the wine's pleasure?*

Bentham suggests some additional considerations for carrying out hedonic calculus:

1. **Intensity:** How strong is the pleasure or pain?
2. **Duration:** How long will the pleasure last?
3. **Certainty** or **uncertainty:** How likely or unlikely is it that the pleasure will occur?
4. **Propinquity:** How soon will the pleasure occur?
5. **Fecundity:** This is the probability that the action will be followed by more pleasure.
6. **Purity:** The probability that the action will not be followed by pain.
7. **Extent:** How many people will be affected?

For example, keeping a promise to do some burdensome task (like babysitting someone's kid sister) will have low **intensity** of pleasure (you get to watch some TV and of course you get paid) with a **duration** of 3-4 hours, compared to going to a friend's party which might have much greater intensity and duration.

The pleasure is pretty **certain**, perhaps more certain than the party (which might be no fun at all if your other friends don't turn up). The **propinquity** is not immediate (you have to entertain the child and put her to bed before you can relax and you won't get paid until the parents return) compared to the party (where you can start enjoying yourself straight away), but the babysitting has **fecundity** (you might be asked to do it again if you get a good reputation) and **purity** (no danger of a hangover the next day).

In terms of **extent**, the babysitting affects you, the parents and the child, but going to the party might affect a larger group of people if your friends are depending on you being there.

Happiness

Bentham uses the phrases 'pleasure' and 'happiness' interchangeably, but later utilitarians made a distinction between the two concepts.

PLEASURE suggests physical wellbeing that is immediate and unreflective: you get pleasure from a nice meal, a hot bath, a cuddle or an upbeat piece of music. The opposite, PAIN or SUFFERING, is a physical sensation or perhaps an intense but short-lived emotion (such as humiliation or fear). There's something rather shallow about pleasure/pain.

HAPPINESS is a more long-lasting state of affairs and a more reflective one: you get happiness from a certain sort of life, from long-term activities or relationships. A person could be in temporary pain but still be happy in the long term. The opposite, UNHAPPINESS or SORROW, is a mental or emotional state that characterises your whole life, so that even moments of pleasure don't stop you being unhappy (for example, alcoholics get short-lived pleasure from drinking, but have unhappy lives).

Later utilitarians like **John Stuart Mill** (p15, 80) moved away from Bentham's analysis and argued that the important thing was to give people a life with a sort of overall positive quality to it – happiness – rather than to offer them short-lived pleasures or spare them short-term pains.

Mill famously illustrates this with a comparison between a philosopher (like Socrates, who strives for happiness) and a pig (who lives for pleasure):

> *It is better to be a human being dissatisfied than a pig satisfied; better to be Socrates dissatisfied than a fool satisfied* – **John Stuart Mill (1863)**

Mill emphasises the QUALITY of happiness as well as the QUANTITY; he argues that there are HIGHER PLEASURES, such as appreciating art, being in long-term relationships and becoming educated which are more valuable than LOWER PLEASURES such as idle entertainment, casual relationships and taking drugs. Mill argues that satisfaction *"of the intellect, of the feelings and imagination, and of the moral sentiments"* are amongst the higher pleasures.

In philosophical terms, Mill moves away from **hedonism** (p11) towards a EUDAIMONISTIC ethical theory. *Eudaimonia* is the Greek word for happiness but it includes the idea of flourishing and wellbeing – of being-all-you-can-be and realizing your potential.

You will study Eudaimonia *in more detail when you consider **Natural Moral Law** (p57) and **Virtue Ethics** in **Topic 5**.*

Social, Political & Cultural Influences

Jeremy Bentham originally proposed Utilitarianism as an attack on the radical idea of **human rights**. Utilitarianism was never intended to be a mere 'theory': it's always been an ethical viewpoint that demands to be put into action.

Utilitarianism suggests that it is the job of the Government to bring about the greatest happiness for the greatest number. This supports democracy, where the Government is elected based on the wishes of the majority of voters.

It's easy to forget just how radical this idea is. Throughout most of human history, rulers have had little interest in doing things that made the majority of people happy. They were largely interested in making themselves happy. The idea that the happiness of a peasant counts for as much as the happiness of a lord was not obvious to everyone (and perhaps still isn't). This is summed up by that great document of the Enlightenment, the **American Declaration of Independence**:

> *We hold these truths to be sacred & undeniable; that all men are created equal & independent, that from that equal creation they derive rights inherent & inalienable, among which are the preservation of life, & liberty, & the pursuit of happiness* – **Thomas Jefferson (1776)**

*The **Declaration of Independence** is a statement of HUMAN RIGHTS, which you will learn about when considering **Natural Mortal Law** (p57) and **Kantian ethics** (c.f. **Topic 5**), but the focus on "the pursuit of happiness" links this to Utilitarianism.*

Utilitarianism was used in the 19th century to justify the abolition of slavery (increasing the happiness of former-slaves) and in the 20th century to support women's suffrage (increasing the happiness of women). However, it was also used to oppose these reforms (warning that the resulting economic turmoil would make everyone, including former slaves, more unhappy or that votes for women would ruin marriages).

In these debates (which are covered in **Topic 1, Environmental Ethics & Equality**), opposition to abolition and women's suffrage turned out to be mistaken but it shows how Utilitarianism can be used to argue either side of most social issues and that calculations about future happiness or unhappiness are full of uncertainty (which is why many campaigners prefer to couch their demands for change in terms of RIGHTS rather than Utilitarianism).

The main influence of Utilitarianism has been as a **justification for punishment**. In traditional ethics, punishment is RETRIBUTIVE because the offender deserves it. Utilitarianism suggests that the am of the punishment should instead be to reduce future crime. This could be through:

- **Deterrence:** Other people, seeing the punishment, will be deterred from offending
- **Protection:** While the criminal is imprisoned, the rest of society is safer
- **Reformation:** The offender will be rehabilitated and will no longer carry out crimes

Retributive punishment focuses on **corporal punishment** (flogging, stocks) or **capital punishment** (executions), utilitarian punishment prefers fines, rehabilitation and community service.

JEREMY BENTHAM

Jeremy Bentham (1748-1832, *c.f.* also p77**)** is a key scholar for Utilitarianism. His contributions include Utilitarianism's focus on **pleasure** (p10), **hedonism** (p11) and link to **act Utilitarianism** (p16) and **negative Utilitarianism** (p19).

He also has an unusual legacy. Radical until the end, Bentham donated his body to science upon his death. His skeleton and head are preserved on display at **University College London**. Bentham's preserved corpse, in his own clothes, is known as the AUTO-ICON and is kept in its own cupboard (*right*). The Auto-Icon is the subject of many student pranks and has, on at least one occasion, attended UCL Council Meetings!

Bentham was a tireless reformer and wrote a huge amount but was not a particularly rigorous philosopher. His ideas on **Psychological Egoism** (p77) are largely rejected and his focus on **pleasure/pain** as the definition of happiness is seen by critics as narrow and superficial.

Nonetheless, Bentham was ahead of his time in seeing the implications of Utilitarianism for sexual equality and animal rights.

Bentham identified a stark difference between his own consequentialist ethics and ethical theories based on HUMAN RIGHTS, such as **Natural Law** (p57) and **Kantian ethics** (*c.f.* **Topic 5**). Bentham was deeply critical of rights-based ethics. This was partly because he didn't think governments could deliver the sort of things that rights-based ethics promised people and partly because he saw how people demanding their rights led to revolution and bloodshed. Bentham believed that Utilitarianism could bring about reform and promote human happiness in a gentler way, without revolution and conflict.

In the 21st century, rights-based ethics are more popular than Utilitarianism (thanks to organizations like the **European Court of Human Rights** and the **U.N. Declaration of Human Rights**). However, it's worth reflecting on Bentham's doubts about rights as the best way to bring about reform, especially after Western invasions of Afghanistan and Iraq in the hope of promoting human rights in those countries.

Nonetheless, rights have been a very effective tool for helping minorities and minorities are often badly served by Utilitarianism. Bringing about the 'greatest happiness' tends to mean giving the majority what they want and the unhappiness of an oppressed minority is just the price that must be paid. There is a failure in Bentham's thinking to engage with the importance of JUSTICE or fairness: a society that is, overall, happy is not necessarily one that treats minority groups fairly.

For example, in recent years the rights of transsexuals have received a lot of attention in Britain. This is a very small minority of people, but promoting their rights has caused indignation and even offence in other communities (for example, traditional Christians). Bentham's Utilitarianism would not support unpopular minorities in situations like this.

JOHN STUART MILL

John Stuart Mill (1806-1873, *c.f.* also p80**)** is a key scholar for Utilitarianism. His contributions include Utilitarianism's focus on **happiness** (p12) and link to **Rule Utilitarianism** (p18).

Like Bentham before him, Mill was a child prodigy who learned Ancient Greek by the time he was three! However, he had a nervous breakdown when he was twenty and this seems to have made him reconsider the purpose of human life and the nature of happiness.

He also married the love of his life **Harriet Taylor (1807-1858)** after a 20-year affair (she was married to another man!) and Harriet's ideas influenced Mill greatly.

Mill's life-changing breakdown and his inspirational (but socially shameful) relationship with Harriet Taylor made him re-think Utilitarianism in a fundamental way.

Unlike Bentham, who took 'pleasure' at face value, Mill understood that, in order to be properly happy, people needed to have a certain overall quality of life and that meant living in a certain sort of society.

> *It is quite compatible with the principle of utility to recognise the fact that some kinds of pleasure are more desirable and more valuable than others –* **J.S. Mill**

Mill's **'higher pleasures'** imply that a person cannot be truly happy in a consistent way unless they have been educated to their full potential, introduced to art and culture and religion and allowed the freedom to express themselves. For example, education is compulsory for teenagers, including things like learning about Shakespeare and foreign languages (which some students find boring or irrelevant); women should have the vote (even if that offends their husbands); minorities in society should be protected and promoted (even if that annoys the majority, because everyone benefits from living in a more diverse and tolerant society).

However, Mill's idea of 'higher pleasures' is **subjective**. Mill took it for granted that appreciating Shakespeare is a higher pleasure (whereas playing a video game is not) but not everyone would agree with this. Similarly, Mill would put classical music above pop music as a higher pleasure. Critics see this as a reflection of Mill's own biases rather than an **objective** difference in the type of pleasure a person gets from (say) Mozart instead of Ariana Grande.

A utilitarian society that maximizes happiness is not necessarily a just or free one. Mill defended the British Empire's colonization of Africa and India, arguing that there were *"barbarians"* who needed *"improvement"* and that it might be justified to take away these people's liberties if it were done *for their own benefit*.

DEVELOPMENT OF UTILITARIANISM

Utilitarianism was first proposed by Bentham in the 18th century and refined by Mill in the 19th century, with Mill's book *Utilitarianism* (1863) being the most complete statement of the theory. Later ethicists added to the theory and refined the ideas that were present in Bentham and Mill's work.

One of the most important was **Henry Sidgwick (1837-1901**, *right*), who published *Methods in Ethics* (1874) in the year after Mill's death. Sidgwick argued for Utilitarianism but addressed several flaws in the ideas of Bentham and Mill, including the question of why a person should sacrifice themselves for the sake of society (**universalistic hedonism**) rather than selfishly seek happiness for themselves or for the people they personally care about (**psychological hedonism**).

Sidgwick adapts **Immanuel Kant's ethical theory** (*c.f.* **Topic 5**) and combines it with Utilitarianism. Sidgwick proposes that, since we have no choice about who we are in a society (we didn't choose our parents, race, social class, gender, etc) it is rational to prefer a society where everybody's happiness is maximized, not just the happiness of a particular group. This makes universalistic hedonism the best Principle of Utility and explains why it is rational to sacrifice your own life and happiness for the sake of strangers (such as a soldier defending his country in war).

Act Utilitarianism

In the 1950s, **Richard Brandt** drew a distinction between two types of Utilitarianism:

- **ACT UTILITARIANISM (AU):** applying the Principle of Utility to each individual action (sometimes termed **direct Utilitarianism** or **extreme Utilitarianism**)
- **RULE UTILITARIANISM (RU):** using the Principe of Utility to determine ethical rules and then following these (sometimes termed **indirect Utilitarianism**)

> *Because this distinction wasn't noticed until the 1950s, earlier utilitarians like **Bentham** and **Mill** tend to veer between the two types. Beware of text books or websites that claim that Bentham was an act utilitarian;* **neither Bentham nor Mill uses these terms**.

An act utilitarian will abandon all ideas about ethical rules. Instead, they approach each situation afresh and make a decision that will maximize overall happiness in that particular situation. In a future situation that is similar in some ways but different in others, they might make a different decision.

For example, an act utilitarian would not accept a general rule against breaking promises. Instead, they would treat each particular promise as a unique situation and work out whether keeping or breaking *that* promise would maximize utility.

Jeremy Bentham's idea of **hedonic calculus** (p11) seems to describe AU at work. However, Bentham was also a campaigner for legal reform, so he clearly thought Utilitarianism could be used to work out ethical rules as well

There are several STRENGTHS of AU. It seems to go to the heart of **consequentialist** thinking (p7) because it rejects the whole idea of **deontological rules** and never puts moral agents in the position of having to do something that will have disastrous consequences when there is another, less harmful option available. This also means it's the type of Utilitarianism that maximizes utility most effectively.

Act utilitarians might agree that there are **'rules of thumb'** that are the correct course of action most of the time: keeping promises is *usually* the right thing to do. However, they would break these rules in a heartbeat, and feel no guilt about it, if a particular promise would have bad consequences (like promising to protect the identity of a murderer).

The main WEAKNESS of AU is that it often **leads to the 'wrong answers'** (answers that go against ordinary conscience). For example, act Utilitarianism seems to approve of executing an innocent man if this satisfies a mob of rioters or deters other criminals; it seems to approve of doctors killing a healthy patient to use the organs to save several other patients (or just *one* other patient who is particularly popular or important).

AU is also criticised for **undermining trust in society**. In a society where everyone were an act utilitarian, promises would have no value and you would never know if anyone was telling you the truth or treating you fairly, because everyone (including you) might turn around and behave antisocially if they calculated this would maximize overall happiness.

> *Think about it: would you marry an act utilitarian? When they're saying their wedding vows "to love and to cherish till death us do part", you know that promise doesn't* **mean** *anything to them and they'd break it to add to all-round happiness (at your expense)!*

It gets even worse if you admit that people are not very good at being **impartial** and tend to be **biased** towards their own happiness (or the happiness of people they care about), often without realising it. Trying to carry out hedonic calculus in an impartial way is difficult and time consuming and might be a **psychological impossibility**.

> *Think about marriage to an act utilitarian again. Can a person make an impartial decision about walking out on their marriage? A lot of cheaters and deserters kid themselves that what they're doing is 'for the best' when it's really just best for* **them**.

Rule Utilitarianism

Richard Brandt (1959, *right*) introduces the idea of **Act Utilitarianism** (p16) but argues in favour of RULE UTILITARIANISM (RU) instead. A rule utilitarian asks, *"What rule would maximize happiness if everyone in the world followed it?"* – then adopts that rule as what Brandt calls a **moral code**.

This means that rule utilitarians act like **deontologists** (p6), except that the rules they follow are based on the Principle of Utility rather than human rights or religious laws.

For example, the human race would be happier overall if everyone kept their promises, therefore a rule utilitarian follows the moral code, *'Always keep your promises!'*

There are several STRENGTHS of RU that are the mirror of act Utilitarianism's weaknesses. RU promotes trust in society, because people follow well-known moral codes involving telling the truth and keeping promises. Wedding vows mean something when a rule utilitarian says them. Most of the moral codes a rule utilitarian follows will be the same as the rules observed by Kantians or proposed by **Natural Law** (p57) – but for different reasons.

RU gets round the problem of people being biased or being unable to perform hedonic calculus quickly and impartially when faced with important decisions. Since *'sticking by your husband/wife and not having affairs'* maximizes utility as a general rule, then that is what a person must do, no matter how unhappy their own marriage makes them or how happy an affair might make them (and their cheating partner, in all likelihood).

Of course, rule utilitarians can admit of **exceptions to rules**. The rule *'stick by your wedding vows'* can have the exception *'unless your spouse is abusing you'* – so long as overall happiness is increased by everyone acting on these exceptions.

The main WEAKNESS of RU is that it **isn't really Utilitarianism at all**! It involves following strict rules like a deontologist – often in situations where there is a clear course of action that would maximise happiness by breaking a rule instead. A rule utilitarian might see that breaking a promise would make lots of people much happier and keeping it would lead to disaster, yet still follow the promise-keeping rule. This seems to go against the original spirit of Utilitarianism as a **consequentialist ethical theory** (p7).

Brandt (1963) defends RU by distinguishing between:

- **STRONG RULE UTILITARIANISM (SRU)** in which the moral codes are **absolute** and are followed **legalistically** (p7)
- **WEAK UTILITARIANISM (WRU)** in which the moral codes have many exceptions are a followed in a flexible way – this is Brandt's preferred type and it resembles **Mill**'s approach to *"secondary principles"* (p80) which can be abandoned when they conflict or confuse

Brandt's WRU is criticised by **David Lyons (1965)** who argues that **weak rule Utilitarianism always collapses into Act Utilitarianism**. This means that the exceptions and sub-rules multiply so much that people cannot keep track of what to do and have to work things out on a case-by-case basis, in which case they are acting as act utilitarians and no longer following ethical rules.

Negative Utilitarianism

Jeremy Bentham argued that, when faced with a choice, a utilitarian should reduce pain first then try to increase pleasure (so feeding a starving man takes priority over throwing a birthday party for a friend). This makes sense as a rule of thumb: a moral person will try to help someone in distress before making the life of an already-happy person even happier.

Karl Popper (1902-1994, *right*) goes beyond this, arguing that reducing unhappiness should *always* be the sole focus for a utilitarian and that adding to happiness is unimportant; this is NEGATIVE UTILITARIANISM (NU):

> *It adds to the clarity of ethics if we formulate our demands negatively, i.e. if we demand the elimination of suffering rather than the promotion of happiness* – **Karl Popper (1952)**

Popper noticed that the Utilitarianism of **Mill** worked comfortably alongside the British Empire and endorsed ruling over colonized peoples 'for their own good' (p15). Popper, who was a fierce defender of democracy against Communism and Fascism, believes that Utilitarianism supports a *"benign dictator"* who takes away people's freedoms in exchange for making them comfortable, wealthy and safe.

> *This argument is made today about the Communist rulers of China, who do not allow democracy or free expression but who have made many Chinese people wealthy and secure. From a normal utilitarian perspective, it might be better to live in a place like China than a democracy like Britain or America, where there is freedom but more inequality.*

Popper rejects the idea of living under a benign dictator, which is the STRENGTH of NU. According to NU, our moral duties extend to removing suffering, hunger and hardship, but we have no moral duty to make people happy: that's up to them to do for themselves. Popper uses the term UTOPIANISM to describe the dangerous attempt by rulers to make people happy:

> *Those who promise us paradise on earth never produced anything but a hell* – **Karl Popper**

Ninian Smart proposed an interesting criticism of NU in a 1958 essay in reply to Popper (in which Smart actually coined the term '**Negative Utilitarianism**' since Popper did not use this term).

Smart points out that a *"benevolent world-exploder"* (a ruler with the weapons instantly to destroy the human race) would have a duty to wipe out all humans, because this would wipe out all suffering. Yes, it would also wipe out all happiness, but happiness is unimportant for NU. Even without a benevolent world-exploder, it has been pointed out that, if everyone were a negative utilitarian, the best action the human race could take would be to commit mass suicide.

One response to this criticism is to argue that NU should accept other utilities beside preventing suffering, such as **Negative Ideal Utilitarianism** (p20) which also values friendship, beauty and knowledge, which would be lost if the human race were wiped out. **Negative Preference Utilitarianism** (p22) would oppose the world-exploder because people are averse to dying.

Australian philosopher **Toby Ord (2013)** outlines the main WEAKNESSES of NU, which can be summed up by saying it is **counter-intuitive** (it goes against our ordinary moral feelings).

- NU suggests a world without happiness is no worse than a happy world, so long as suffering has been prevented. Contrary to NU, most people feel that it's better to be happy than mediocre.
- Most people believe in trade-offs and are prepared to accept a certain amount of suffering in order to achieve some happiness, like hitting the gym to lose weight or spending the weekend revising to get good exam results. NU seems to suggest that suffering (or boredom) can never be justified by the happiness it produces later.
- NU suggests that efforts to add to your own (or other people's) happiness are not worthwhile: there's no value in sending people birthday cards, going to the movies or cooking nice meals. Only preventing suffering matters, like ending world hunger or solving the Israel-Palestine problem.

Ideal Utilitarianism

Some utilitarians criticise the idea that utility is the same as pleasure or hedonism. **G.E. Moore (1873-1958)** points out that there are malicious pleasures, like spite. He imagines two universes: one that is empty of life and one inhabited only by sadists. For Bentham, all pleasure is good, but Moore argues that the empty universe is better than the sadistic one.

Moore proposes that there are **non-hedonic goods**: things *other than pleasure* that give value to actions. These are:

- **Friendship**
- **Aesthetic enjoyment** (the experience of beauty)
- Acquiring **knowledge**

A utilitarian like Bentham would reply that these experiences are **instrumentally good** (friendship makes us happy, as do art and finding things out) but Moore argues that these experiences are *a different sort of thing* from pleasure because they depend on the object of your experience *actually existing*.

- **Friendship** can be faked. For Bentham, there is no difference between the pleasure you get from a true friendship or merely believing you have a friend, even though that person secretly despises you or is not what they seem. For Moore, true friendship has a value of its own.
- **Aesthetic enjoyment** can be mistaken, if you are admiring a fake work of art. Again, this makes no difference on Bentham's view, but Moore argues that it matters that you are enjoying the *real Mona Lisa* in the Louvre in Paris, not a fake or a printed copy.
- Acquiring **knowledge** can also be deluded, such as 'fake news' on the Internet or propaganda from governments. For Bentham, believing comforting lies is better than learning unpleasant truths, but Moore argues that learning the truth about things has value even if it makes you unhappy.

Moore's ideas were developed by **Hastings Rashdall (1858-1924)** who uses the term IDEAL UTILITARIANISM (IU) for a Principle of Utility based on **several competing non-hedonic goods besides pleasure** that have to be balanced against each other.

The main STRENGTH of IU is that it makes an important distinction between **real versus delusional pleasures**. People sometimes live in a 'fool's paradise': for example, a person may be ignorant that their partner is cheating on them, that their so-called friend is using them for their money or that the items they are excited about collecting are really valueless junk. Is it ethical to alert people to the truth of their situation, if it makes them very unhappy?

IU says that it's better to know the truth. The theory also argues that it's better to read actual books rather than take in Wikipedia summaries or movie adaptations; better to visit actual places rather than view them through your computer on Google Maps; and better to have real experiences rather than live in a virtual reality world.

The WEAKNESS of IU is that, while the value of pleasure is agreed by everyone, the value of non-hedonic goods is much more **subjective**. Not everyone enjoys art and some people don't seem to need friends in their life. Other non-hedonic goods can be suggested, like religious worship (especially if God exists), sporting activity (which is often painful) or romantic love (which can also be faked): the list goes on.

The central appeal of Utilitarianism is that it reduces ethical decision-making to a simple calculation about pleasure, but IU leads to much more complicated decisions involving an unclear list of competing goods.

However, IU can be combined with **Negative Utilitarianism** (p19). Negative-IU argues that, rather than promote friendship, beauty and knowledge/truth, we should work to reduce or remove hatred, ugliness and ignorance/lies. This is a bit easier to define than normal IU and it also forms a counter-argument to **Smart**'s *"benevolent world exploder"* (p20) who would remove all suffering by killing the human race: this mass killing would not remove ugliness/ignorance and would probably increase it.

Preference Utilitarianism

Another **non-hedonic** type of Utilitarianism is PREFERENCE UTILITARIANISM (PU). PU proposes that utility should be defined as **maximizing the satisfaction of preferences**; in other words, ensuring that as many people as possible get as much of what they want as possible.

As with other types of utility (such as pleasure or happiness), it's the *overall* satisfaction of preferences that matters and the *identity* of the preference-holder is unimportant. This means everyone's preferences count equally and majority preferences (or strongly held ones) outweigh minority preferences (or weakly held ones).

For example, if I borrow money from a friend, my friend has a preference that I pay her back but I might have a preference not to. Maybe my preference outweighs my friend's (if I am poor and the money means a lot to me and she is rich and doesn't miss it); however, lots of other people might prefer to see debts repaid in general, perhaps most people in society prefer debts to be repaid. Therefore I satisfy most preferences by repaying the money, even though it goes against my own preferences.

PU is discussed by **Henry Sidgwick** and promoted by the English philosopher **R.M. Hare** but it is mostly associated today with Hare's student, the Australian philosopher **Peter Singer** (*right*).

> *An action contrary to the preference of any being is, unless this preference is outweighed by contrary preferences, wrong –* **Peter Singer (1993)**

> *Singer has recently distanced himself from PU, but his name is so firmly associated with it in every textbook and website that you should cite him as the principle scholar for this theory in your essays.*

There are several STRENGTHS for PU compared to other types of Utilitarianism. It avoids the problem identified by Popper, since so long as people prefer to be free and democratic, a "*benign dictator*" (p19) can never be in the right, no matter how happy he makes people.

> *But what if the benign dictator is popular and people prefer his rule to being free? Nearly 1.4 billion people live in China and most of them seem to prefer Communist rule. Or, to take a different example, in the 1930s, the German people mostly preferred Nazism. There's a problem here for people like Popper who value freedom and democracy and worry that Utilitarianism does not protect it.*

PU offers a solution to Smart's "*benevolent world exploder*" (p20) because people prefer not to die – or, if we adopt **Negative-PU**, we should reduce the things people are averse to and people are usually averse to dying, even if they are living lives of great hardship.

PU also has implications for animal rights (*c.f.* **Topic 1**). Psychologists debate whether animals of different types experience suffering or unhappiness, but there can be no doubt that they have preferences – they prefer not to be killed and eaten and there are lots of them so their preferences might outweigh the preferences of humans to have meat in their diet.

PU gets round the problem of defining 'happiness' (p12) and higher/lower pleasures because it treats all preferences the same: preferences for drugs and violent video games are just the same as preferences for nature walks and classical music. However, preferences for antisocial or destructive things go against the wider preferences of people in society as a whole, so even if you prefer to lie on the couch drinking and playing violent video games, you are outnumbered by your parents, teachers, workmates and neighbours who would prefer you didn't.

There are WEAKNESSES of PU. It seems to dignify perverse or futile preferences just as much as sophisticated and high-minded ones: strange hobbies (like collecting shoelaces) satisfy preferences as much as reading great literature. This is linked to the problem that people do not know what is really in their own best interests, so what they prefer might be in conflict with what they really need. Many people prefer to eat sugary junk food and gamble but they would be better off following a healthy diet and saving money. Some might argue that whatever people *think* they prefer, they *really* prefer to be healthy and wealthy and they should be prevented from gorging on pizza and betting on horses. However, this seems to go against the central appeal of PU, which is that it replaces complicated calculations about happiness with a fairly straightforward analysis of what people say they want.

Related to this is the distinction between short term and long term preferences. In the short term, I might prefer to go to parties every night but in the long term I prefer to do well in my studies and career. Should a friend or family member encourage me in satisfying my immediate preferences (by throwing a party) or encourage me in my long-term ones (by insisting I stay home and work), even though it will be frustrating for me right now?

Other critics focus on the problem of infinite preferences: these are preferences that overrule everything else. For example, a religious teetotaler has an infinite preference that people do not drink alcohol: it's simply the most important thing in the world to them. I have a mild preference for a glass of wine with my evening meal. Does the teetotaler's infinite preference overrule the lesser ('finite') preferences of all the other people who like to drink alcohol on occasions?

Relativism in Ethics

Relativism is the idea that there is no objective right or wrong: morality is relative to each person and each situation.

- MORAL RELATIVISM proposes that each individual has their own sense of ethics which is true for them but not for other people
- CULTURAL RELATIVISM proposes that each community or society has its own moral code which is true for its members but not for outsiders

In some ways, Utilitarianism is a relativist ethical theory. Because we, as individuals, find different things pleasurable, what maximizes happiness for one person might not maximize it for another. Happiness is therefore relative. Similarly, different cultures take pleasure from different things: bullfighting in Spain, eating frogs' legs in France, baseball in America, cricket in the UK. Therefore things that maximize happiness in one country will not work in another.

On the other hand, Utilitarianism can be seen as **non-relativist**. For a utilitarian, it is objectively true that 'good' means the greatest happiness for the greatest number. This is true for everyone. It's not the case that happiness is important for some people but not for others, or that there are cultures which value happiness but others that don't. **Jeremy Bentham** writes that "*Nature has placed mankind under the governance of two sovereign masters, pain and pleasure.*" Bentham means that pleasure has ultimate utility for all of mankind and that this state of affairs is natural, not a cultural trend that can be changed.

> *There might be people who don't **admit** that they value happiness or cultures that encourage people to despise happiness. However, the things they recommend instead (say, patriotism or hard work or praying all the time) are things that make them happy, so a utilitarian would say these people value happiness without realising it.*

Of course, utilitarians disagree about how 'greatest happiness' is to be defined. **Ideal utilitarians** (p20) think there are other goods that have utility besides happiness (friendship, beauty, knowledge) but they too think these things are objectively good for everyone, all over the world (non-relativist) while admitting that different people might look for different things in friendship, art or education. **Preference utilitarians** (p22) think that satisfying preferences has utility. Once again, they agree that satisfaction of preferences is objectively good for everyone everywhere while admitting that everyone has their own unique set of preferences that are shaped by the culture they live in.

An **act utilitarian** would tend towards **cultural relativism**. For example, they would oppose female genital mutilation (FGM) in the UK because the number of people made happy by it is very small compared to the number of people who are outraged by it. However, they don't live by a rule which says "*No FGM!*" and if they found themselves in a country where it was popular (e.g. in the Horn of Africa) then their personal outrage would count for little against the majority who were made happy by the practice, so they would have to approve of it.

Many philosophers oppose relativism in ethics, because it seems to disallow anyone from criticising anyone else – or at least, it disallows people from one culture from criticising people from another culture. It stands in contrast to the idea of HUMAN RIGHTS that cuts across all cultures and imposes a standard everyone is expected to live up to. The tendency of some utilitarians to support relativism counts as a criticism of Utilitarianism for many people.

EVALUATING UTILITARIANISM

The main strength of Utilitarianism is that it isn't **deontology** (p6): it's flexible, responsive to situations and it doesn't commit moral agents to destructive courses of behaviour simply because *'those are the rules!'* It offers solutions to ethical problems (such as the **Trolley Problem**, p8) that are, for many people, highly INTUITIVE – Utilitarianism often agrees with our moral feelings that consequences matter and that it's better to be happy than sad.

There are many criticisms:

- **PLEASURE IS NOT THE ONLY GOOD:** Hedonism focuses only on pleasure but many people believe there are **non-hedonic goods** like justice, freedom or the right to life. Without these, Utilitarianism is in danger of supporting **Popper's Benign Dictator** (p19) who offers to make people happy at the cost of taking away their freedom. **Ideal Utilitarianism** (p20) incorporates non-hedonic goods (friendship, beauty and knowledge).

- **PSYCHOLOGICAL IMPOSSIBILITY:** Bentham's **hedonic calculus** (p11) seems to be hard to carry out because the future consequences of our behaviour are not known. It's particularly hard to weigh up all possible outcomes 'on the spur of the moment'. Utilitarians reply that this criticism is overstated: we go through life weighing up likely consequences all the time and not many moral decisions have to be taken in a hurry. **Rule Utilitarians** (p18) don't have to make 'spur of the moment' decisions.

- **SHORT-TERM THINKING:** Bentham's principles of **Certainty & Propinquity** (p11) prefer actions that deliver happiness in the short term rather than uncertain long term happiness. However, many problems facing the planet in the 21st century seem to require long term thinking. **Peter Singer** admits that **Preference Utilitarianism** (p22) fails to deal with environmental problems because it favours the current generation using the Earth's resources rather than conserving them for future generations whose wishes we cannot be certain about (*c.f.* **Topic 1 Environmental Ethics**).

- **'WRONG' ANSWERS:** Utilitarianism has no way of taking into account people's rights or basic dignity; the whole point is that some people's interests are sacrificed for the sake of others (as can be seen in the way utilitarians solve the **Trolley Problem** by killing one worker so that five can live). Utilitarianism seems to justify doctors killing patients for their organs and judges punishing the innocent to deter criminals. **Negative Utilitarianism** (p19) is a solution to some of these problems but it invites its own problems (such as **Smart's Benevolent World-Exploder**, p20).

Two objections to Utilitarianism need to be considered in detail.

Actual vs Foreseeable Consequences

J.C.C. ("Jack") Smart (1949, the brother of **Ninian Smart**, p20) distinguishes ACTUAL and FORESEEABLE CONSEQUENCES. Should a utilitarian judge actions by their actual consequences (the amount of happiness actually created) or the consequences the person could foresee at the time (which might be mistaken)?

'Foreseeable consequences' allows us to say that a person did the right thing but it turned out badly: their intentions were good. However, this seems very similar to problems with **deontology**, where a person follows moral rules with good intentions but produces terrible consequences. Utilitarianism is supposed to avoid this.

'Actual consequences' holds people accountable for the consequences of their actions: if you cause suffering, you did the wrong thing and your intentions are irrelevant. However, this produces the odd conclusion that we cannot know the moral character of our actions until after we have done them, possibly a long time after.

- If you rescue a child from drowning, you might think you did a good thing, but if that child grows up to be a murderer or warlord then you actually did a bad thing
- If you drive carelessly and kill a pedestrian, you might think you did a bad thing, but if you killed a murderer on his way to commit his crime then what you did was actually good

By contrast, **deontology** offers people the clear understanding that they are doing the right thing or the wrong thing at the time that they do it.

The Experience Requirement

Utilitarianism struggles to evaluate situations where somebody does not experience pain or unhappiness, even though they are clearly being wronged. This happens when you are hurt without realizing it (e.g. when someone cheats or cons you) or when you are deluded (e.g. when you think someone loves you but they don't). It includes types of evil that people don't experience as pain or unhappiness, such as the death of the last member of an endangered species in a remote jungle somewhere, without anyone hearing about it.

The clearest example of this is the Peeping Tom who spies on a woman while she undresses. The voyeur (wicked observer) gets a lot of pleasure from doing this; ordinarily that would be canceled out by the intense shame and indignation of his victim, however in this case the victim does not **know** she is being spied upon and so experiences no unhappiness.

This leads to the odd conclusion that the voyeur is doing nothing wrong **so long as** his victim never finds out. For many critics, this perverse conclusion shows that there is something wrong with Utilitarianism.

But not with **all** types of Utilitarianism.

- **Rule Utilitarianism** (p18) would formulate a rule of '*No Peeping Toms*' because this is a rule which, if everyone followed it, would maximise happiness.
- **Negative Utilitarianism** (p19) would pay no attention to the voyeur's pleasure and pay attention only to reducing unhappiness, which in this case means the woman's possible distress were she to find out counts for more than the voyeur's pleasure.
- **Preference Utilitarianism** (p22) would acknowledge the voyeur's preference to spy but also the woman's preference **not** to be spied upon along with a similar preference by **all** women not to be spied upon (and doubtless a preference for this by their families and partners too) which easily outweighs the voyeur's wishes.

Compatibility with religious approaches

Jeremy Bentham and **John Stuart Mill** were both hostile towards religious morality. Bentham argues that an all-loving God, if he existed, would surely be a utilitarian (he would want to make all his creatures as happy as possible), but, since there is excessive suffering in the world, this shows that there is something wrong with the concept of the Christian God.

> *This is the **Problem of Evil & Suffering** that you study in **Unit 1 (Philosophy & Religion)**. Notice t*
> *Bentham's conclusion is not the only option: it's possible that the coexistence of suffering and a lo*
> *God shows that there is something wrong with Utilitarianism.*

Despite this, there are clear connections between Utilitarianism and religious ethics. Loving someone involves promoting their happiness and Christianity urges this:

> *Love your neighbor as yourself* – **Matthew 22: 39**

> *Do to others what you would have them do to you* – **Matthew 7: 12**

These sentiments resemble Utilitarianism's principle of counting other people's happiness as equal to your own.

However, Christian ethics also have a focus on the SANCTITY OF LIFE, with each person's life having infinite value. This does not allow the sort of trade-offs that Utilitarianism can make. Fr example, in the **Trolley Problem** (p8) a utilitarian calculates that 5 lives are worth more happiness than one, but a Christian might believe that one person's life to be of infinite value therefore it is wrong to kill him or her, even in order to save other people.

Religions like Christianity also recognise some lives as having special moral value, such as the poor or innocent children. A utilitarian might see little difference between adding to the happiness of a beggar or a wealthy person, but for a Christian the beggar's happiness is more important than the wealthy person's.

Religious ethics also stress the motives of the moral agent. For a utilitarian, motives are unimportant and only consequences matter, but for a religious believer, God sees and judges for your motives:

> *What good will it be for someone to gain the whole world, yet forfeit their soul?* – **Matthew 16: 26**

From a religious perspective, thought and feelings can be evil even if you never act on them.

> *Anyone who looks at a woman lustfully has already committed adultery with her in hi. heart* – **Matthew 5: 28**

Whereas for a utilitarian thoughts that never get acted upon don't matter since they don't actually contribute to making anyone happy or sad:

Because of these differences, religious ethics usually oppose Utilitarianism and support **deontology** (p6), **Natural Moral Law** (pX57 and **virtue ethics** (*c.f.* **Topic 5**).

...TION OF UTILITARIANISM

...ecification asks students to discuss

...plication of the theory in historical and contemporary ethical situations, including
...al and social reform

...oints have already been covered in the earlier sections, but I shall bring them
...under the two categories identified in the Specification.

Ethical Situations

...was developed by **Jeremy Bentham** (p14, 77) to encourage the reforming work of
...ent

...ng the power of religious beliefs and churches over law and politics
...ting **democracy** and **egalitarianism** (equality) among people
...ng a **rational** and **scientific** outlook

...d that Utilitarianism would promote these things without the revolutions and
... (he believed) the theory of HUMAN RIGHTS had encouraged in France and
...am hoped Utilitarianism would bring about equality for women and better
...nimals.

...ll (p15, 80) saw the abolition of slavery as being in line with utilitarian thinking.
...he promoted the equality of women. However, he did not see Utilitarianism as
...perialism or **colonialism** as the British Empire dominated whole nations in Africa
...eir own good'.

...ial Reform

...ms in Britain and America abolished slavery and then extended the FRANCHISE
...:e) to more men and then women. These developments were influenced by
...:

...abolished slavery in its Empire in 1833. In the USA, the Thirteenth Amendment
...ed slavery in 1865.
...n, three Reform Acts in the 19th century **extended the franchise to more men**
... wealthy landowners: the 1832 Reform Act gave the vote to hundreds of
...ds of homeowners; the 1867 doubled the voting population by including a million
...;; the 1884 Act tripled the number of voters, which now included most men.
...MEN'S SUFFRAGE MOVEMENT campaigned for **women to be able to vote**, which
...wed for some women in 1918 and extended to all British women in 1928. In the
...e Nineteenth Amendment extended the franchise to American women in 1919.

Utilitarian ideas about maximizing happiness influenced these reforms but Utilitarianism was also used to argue *against* reform. For example, it was argued that abolishing slavery would increase unhappiness by ruining the economy for everyone, that equality for women would lead to conflict in marriages and that extending the franchise to uneducated men would destroy the 'higher pleasures' of art and culture. Most of these fears weren't realised, but (along with Mill's support for Empire), they show that Utilitarianism does not *always* have positive applications.

Contemporary Ethical Situations

Utilitarianism has declined in significance in modern politics and legal reform. This is partly because reform is increasingly concerned with promoting the freedoms of minority groups whose small numbers don't have much influence in **hedonic calculus** (p11), especially when the majority of the population is unsympathetic to their case. Instead, the idea of HUMAN RIGHTS is more commonly used to protect these groups:

- Homosexuality was decriminalised in 1967 and the **Equality Act (2010)** banned discrimination against LGBT people. **Same-sex marriage** was legalised in 2013.
- Hate crimes were identified and banned by the **Criminal Justice Act (2003)**: as well as racism this reform bans persecuting people for their religion or their subculture (like Goths).
- The UK Government is considering legislation to ban **Islamophobia** but this is proving more controversial, due to disagreements in the definition of the term.

Political & Social Reform

There are two areas of modern life where Utilitarianism still promotes reform. One is ANIMAL RIGHTS (*c.f.* **Topic 1 Environmental Ethics**) where a concern for animal suffering has led to campaigns for vegetarianism and veganism, an end to animal experimentation, banning blood sports and concerns about animals in zoos.

The other is Mill's **Harm Principle** (p80) which promotes the LIBERALISATION of the law (i.e. making things legal that used to be banned, based on the argument that no one is harmed by doing these things). This has led to more relaxed laws on pornography, gambling and recreational drugs as well as access to divorce for ordinary people.

However, the Harm Principle has also led to some things that used to be legal becoming banned in the interest of public safety and reducing suffering. An obvious example is owning guns but this also includes driving without a seatbelt, owning dangerous dogs and (in Scotland and Wales but not yet in England) smacking your children.

In politics, Utilitarianism promotes the view that **each person should have equal political importance**. That has been used to criticise the HOUSE OF LORDS, which used to include anyone who inherited a title. However, this was changed in 1999 so that only 92 'hereditary peers' get to sit in the House of Lords; the rest have to be appointed by the Government. Attempts to change the voting system to PROPORTIONAL REPRESENTATION have not been successful so far.

Changes to Social Attitudes

When **Bentham** and **Mill** proposed utilitarian ideas, they were criticised for valuing happiness so highly instead of traditional morals like justice, mercy, loyalty or freedom. Such criticisms are much less common today: the **hedonic** basis of Utilitarianism has become mainstream.

For example, since 2012, INTERNATIONAL DAY OF HAPPINESS is celebrated annually with a report that measures happiness in 156 countries. In 2019, the UK is 15th, ahead of Germany (17th) and the USA (19th) but Finland, Denmark and Norway are the happiest nations.

This concern with maximizing happiness can be seen in the growth of WELBEING as a state that business and schools want to promote in employees or young people. There are apps to measure wellbeing and courses for meditation and mindfulness that increase wellbeing. In 2014, the UK Government began a project to measure national wellbeing after scientific reports linked happiness to health, long life and more positive social contributions.

This is linked to increasingly LIBERAL social attitudes, which believe that people should be allowed to do things that make them happy, particularly if those things don't make other people unhappy. This can be seen in increasing tolerance for recreational drug use, alternative sexual orientations and gender identities that used to be strongly condemned.

It's not clear whether Utilitarianism itself has promoted these social attitudes or whether these attitudes along with Utilitarianism are all the result of changes that have been going on since the Enlightenment: increasing focus on the individual in society, more leisure time and the decline of religion bringing more of a focus on this life rather than the Afterlife.

Peter Vardy (2009) argues that the rise of Utilitarianism has caused a moral crisis in Western culture, leading to a TRANSACTIONAL view of sex (based on giving and receiving pleasure) that leaves no room for commitment and deeper feelings.

> *Vardy is a Key Scholar for **Topic 3.2 (Sexual Ethics)** and his critique of Utilitarian attitudes to sex is a Socially Conservative view. Other writers celebrate the freedom to live life your own way occasioned by Utilitarianism*

TOPIC 2.2 SITUATION ETHICS

Situation Ethics (SE) is an ethical theory that tries to position itself between **consequentialism** (p7) and **deontology** (p6). It tries to keep some of the stability and certainty of deontological ethics but incorporate some of the flexibility and nuance of consequentialism.

Some times we get impatient with rules or working out the consequences of our actions and we say that, surely, it's the *thought* that counts? This is a view of ethics based on MOTIVES rather than duties or consequences. Most people agree that the best motive in the world is loving kindness, which is why this approach is sometimes called AGAPEIC ethics, from the Greek word *agápē* (selfless love).

SE emerged during a difficult time for religious ethics in Europe and America. After World War II, a new sort of society emerged with very different views on right and wrong from previous generations. This outlook, which became mainstream among many young people in the 1960s, is known as the NEW MORALITY and SE is a response to it.

But what exactly is the New Morality?

The 'New Morality'

For centuries, Christian morality was seen by millions of people as the best morality, and being a good Christian meant following the rules laid out in the Bible (especially the Ten Commandments) and the rules laid down by the church (such as not having sex before marriage or getting divorced). This started to change during the Enlightenment when writers and thinkers questioned the purity of Christian morality or the goodness of the church's rules.

- Christian leaders had enthusiastically tortured and executed people for being **heretics and witches**
- Christians had waged war on Muslims during the **Crusades** (11th to 13th centuries)
- Catholic and Protestant Christians had waged war on each other during the **European Wars of Religion** in the 16th and 17th centuries

The phrase **'New Morality'** was coined by the American philosopher **Durant Drake** in his 1928 book of the same name. Drake observes changes in attitudes after World War I and predicts the end of the old Christian value-system. The 'Roaring Twenties' was a time of growing LIBERALISM, with more acceptance of behaviour that had been considered immoral previously:

- Women gained the vote and began working and attending university in large numbers
- Black culture, particularly jazz music, became more mainstream
- Sexual experimentation (such as homosexuality or living together outside of marriage) became less taboo

The 1960s was another time of great cultural and social change, brought on by the BABY BOOMERS (children born in the years after World War II) growing up into teenagers and creating a PERMISSIVE SOCIETY inspired by individualism, rock music and free expression:

- The Women's Liberation movement challenged the role of women in society, especially in traditional marriages
- The Anti-War Movement questioned the old values of duty and patriotism
- People started to experiment with recreational drugs and non-marital sex, with some advocating 'FREE LOVE' (sex without any commitments)

Many people saw this New Morality as based on peace and tolerance and rejecting religious rules. Religious believers were divided in how to respond to the New Morality:

- **CONSERVATIVES** believed in sticking to the old-fashioned rules and disapproved of the "**permissive society**" going on around them

  This is not a new morality—this is the old immorality – **Billy Graham (evangelist preacher)**

- **LIBERALS** thought that the New Morality was making some good points and wanted to adapt Christian teachings to include them

*You may ask yourself whether the liberal believers **really** agreed with the New Morality on sex outside marriage, drugs and pacificism – or if they were just adopting popular new views to stop their churches from becoming irrelevant. The 'Trendy Vicar' who encourages liberal views that go against traditional Christian teachings is a joke figure for many people.*

Social, Political & Cultural Influences

The New Morality is based on the assumption that happiness is the greatest good and nothing should stand in the way of this. It is therefore a EUDAIMONIC (happiness-based) ethic.

This is partly influenced by political LIBERALISM and **J.S. Mill's Harm Principle** (p80) which proposes that people should be allowed to do whatever makes them happy so long as it doesn't make other people unhappy. Liberal thinking led to more relaxed attitudes towards sex, drugs and free expression and changes in the law regarding homosexuality and divorce in the 1960s.

The psychologist **Sigmund Freud (1856-1939,** *right***)** helped to change attitudes with books like ***Civilisation and its Discontents* (1930)**. Freud argues that it is healthy to express instincts, even ones that society considers shameful and wrong, and unhealthy to **repress** them.

Freud regards sex as the fundamental motivator in human behaviour and views guilt/shame as symptoms of mental disorder. The goal of healthy human living is to accept these feelings, not deny them or reject them as traditional Christian ethics would encourage you to do.

However, living in society forces us to deny our pleasures and feel shame. For Freud, society itself is neurotic (ill).

Freud's theories are largely discredited in Psychology, but his ideas have been very influential with the public. Freudianism claims that healthy behaviour is good and unhealthy behaviour is bad: the healthiest behaviour is to **express your instinctive wishes and desires** in a way that is safe and (according to the **Harm Principle**) doesn't hurt anyone else.

An invention linked to these changes is the CONTRACEPTIVE PILL. 'The Pill' was introduced in Britain on the NHS in 1961, but only to married women who had already had children, because the Government did not want to be seen as encouraging 'Free Love' and casual sex.

The Pill was controversial from the start. **Pope Paul VI** condemned the use of the Pill by Catholics in his encyclical ***Humanae Vitae* (1968)**.

In 1974, family planning clinics started issuing the Pill to unmarried women. Today, it is estimated that 70% of all women in Britain have used the Pill at some stage in their lives (**source: BBC, 2011**). This intensifies the criticism that the Pill promotes PROMISCUITY (sexual immorality).

The Pill certainly removed the fear of unwanted pregnancy from sex. In the 1960s, fewer that 1% of couples COHABITED (lived together without being married) but today 1 in 6 do. The Pill also helped develop the view that sex is for pleasure rather than for procreation (producing children). When this is combined with the **Harm Principle**, any sort of sex becomes morally acceptable so long as all parties in the act CONSENT to it.

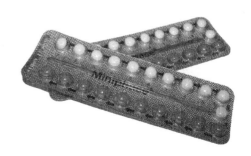

However, critics argue that the Pill has led to the rise of STIs (Sexually Transmitted Infections). Moreover, a culture of CASUAL SEX is blamed for making women vulnerable to rape and (when contraception fails, as it occasionally does) increasing both abortions and children growing up without a father present in their lives.

> *These examples focus on sexual behaviour because that is the aspect of the New Morality that attracts the most attention and debate. Notice that – except for **Durant Drake** (p31) – the New Morality is not really a coherent moral code. It's more of an outlook or sensibility that makes a lot of traditional moral ideas* **feel** *silly and pointless.*

Christian thinkers struggled to apply traditional moral ideas to a changing society. One of the main texts in Situation Ethics is **John Robinson's *Honest To God* (1963, p81).** John Robinson was the Bishop of Woolwich and his book threw the Church into turmoil by arguing that Christianity needed to *embrace* aspects of the New Morality. In place of all the religious rules, Robinson argued there was only one moral law: THE LAW OF LOVE.

The *"law of Love"* is not a new idea - it is based on much older ideas within Christianity. The New Testament uses the Greek word ***AGÁPĒ*** (pronounced *ah-guh-pay*), which used to be translated as "charity" but means **selfless, compassionate love**.

AGAPE IN ETHICS

Love has always been a popular basis for Christian ethics. Because God is Omniscient (All-Knowing), he is aware, not only of our actions, but of our intentions. Christian thinkers have declared that God judges people based on their intentions as much as (maybe more than) the things they actually **do**.

For example, Jesus claims that someone who just thinks about adultery is as guilty as someone who actually committed it (**Matthew 5: 27-28**).

Thomas Aquinas (p76) also made a distinction between EXTERIOR ACTS (the things we physically do) and INTERIOR ACTS (the things we decide to do) and argues that interior acts are more morally important. For example, we don't tend to admire people who do good things by accident, or reluctantly, or because they were trying to impress us – we're much more impressed with people who *try* to do the right thing, even if their attempt goes wrong. We say things like, *"Never mind, your heart was in the right place"*.

For centuries, Christianity has encouraged *IMITATIO DEI*, living your life in imitation of Jesus or God. Several Christian writers in the 20th century returned to this idea as a way of cutting through ethical dilemmas:

> There is only one ultimate and invariable duty, and its formula is 'Thou shalt love thy neighbour as thyself" – **William Temple (1917)**

> The law of love is the ultimate law because it is the negation of law – **Paul Tillich (1951)**

Tillich's comment is particularly interesting, because he makes a contrast between ethics that are based on *"law"* (meaning **deontology**, lists of *do*s and *don't*s) and ethics that are based on love.

The idea of **the 'Law of Love'** as the basis for ethics inspired **Joseph Fletcher (1905-1991**, *right* and p78) to develop **Situation Ethics** or **Situationalism**. Situationalism proposes that:

- In exceptional circumstances, **ordinary moral laws can be broken**
- The Law of Love instructs us **when moral laws no longer apply**: when it would *no longer be the loving thing to do*
- The Law of Love provides guidance for **what to do in these situations**: *do the most loving thing*

Fletcher and Robinson both argue that AGAPEIC ETHICS (following the Law of Love) offers a way of dealing with ethical problems that is much close to what the Bible recommends than the **deontological** moral rules that are usually taken to be 'Christian ethics'.

Biblical examples of Situationalism in ethics

The idea of *agápē* goes right back to the beginnings of Christianity in the writings of **St Paul**. Writing to the Christians in Corinth (probably in the 50s CE), Paul insists they put aside their differences and show compassionate, selfless love for each other:

> *If I speak in the tongues of men or of angels, but do not have AGÁPĒ, I am only a resounding gong or a clanging cymbal. If I have the gift of prophecy and can fathom all mysteries and all knowledge, and if I have a faith that can move mountains, but do not have AGÁPĒ, I am nothing. If I give all I possess to the poor and give over my body to hardship that I may boast, but do not have AGÁPĒ, I gain nothing* – **1 Corinthians 13: 1-3**

This passage is often read at weddings with *agápē* translated as 'love' – it is part of the famous '*Love is...*' passage.

> *AGÁPĒ is patient, AGÁPĒ is kind. It does not envy, it does not boast, it is not proud. It does not dishonour others, it is not self-seeking, it is not easily angered, it keeps no record of wrongs. AGÁPĒ does not delight in evil but rejoices with the truth. It always protects, always trusts, always hopes, always perseveres. AGÁPĒ never fails* – **1 Corinthians 4-8**

Despite the weddings-connection, it is important to be very clear that *agápē* is **not** romantic love: it's not about hearts, kisses or powerful emotions. It's not the sort of love you feel for your wife or husband or your children or your friends.

- It's a **choice**, not a feeling
- It's something you **do**, not something that happens to you
- It's directed at people who **need** help, not people who **deserve** help

> *The biggest problem for students writing about Situation Ethics is that the word 'love' in English has so many romantic associations. You have to get that out of your head. The Biblical idea of AGÁPĒ is the love that God has for humans and that Christians try to imitate. It's detached and rational and deliberate. It's about CHOOSING what's best for others. There's nothing sentimental or romantic about it.*

The Bible states that *agápē* is the very nature of God:

> *God is Love (Theos agápē estin)* – **I John 4:8**

This means that *agápē* isn't just a human feeling. It isn't a product of hormones or brain structure or millions of years of evolution. Selfless compassionate love is the fundamental law of the universe. When you show *agápē* towards other human beings, you are behaving like God. *Agápē* transcends ordinary moral rules like keeping promises, sparing lives or doing your duty.

The Ministry of Jesus

Jesus' 'Ministry' is the period he spent teaching and preaching before his 'Passion' (his arrest and Crucifixion). *Agápē* seems to be at the heart of Jesus' Ministry. Jesus says that his **'New Commandment'** is that his disciples should "*love one another* (agapate allēlous)" (**John 13: 34**).

Jesus recommends *agápē* on many occasions. When his followers asked him which is the **Greatest Commandment**, Jesus replies:

> *Love the Lord your God with all your heart and with all your soul and with all your mind.'*
> *This is the first and greatest commandment. And the second is like it: 'Love your*
> *neighbour (agapēsies ton plēsion) as yourself.' All the Law and the Prophets hang on*
> *these two commandments* – **Matthew 22: 37-40**

The most striking example of Jesus illustrating the Law of Love would be **the story of the woman caught in adultery** – also known as the *Pericope Adulterae*. 'Adultery' is sex involving a married woman and someone who is not her husband (or in this case, perhaps, not her fiancé) and this is condemned by the 7th of the Ten Commandments: *You shall not commit adultery* (**Exodus 20: 14**).

The teachers of the law and the Pharisees brought in a woman caught in adultery. They made her stand before the group and said to Jesus, "Teacher, this woman was caught in the act of adultery. In the Law, Moses commanded us to stone such women. Now what do you say?" They were using this question as a trap, in order to have a basis for accusing him.

But Jesus bent down and started to write on the ground with his finger. When they kept on questioning him, he straightened up and said to them, "Let any one of you who is without sin be the first to throw a stone at her."

Again he stooped down and wrote on the ground.

At this, those who heard began to go away one at a time, the older ones first, until only Jesus was left, with the woman still standing there. Jesus straightened up and asked her, "Woman, where are they? Has no one condemned you?"

"No one, sir," *she said.*

"Then neither do I condemn you," *Jesus declared.* "Go now and leave your life of sin." – **John 8: 3-11**

Jesus seems to reject following the Jewish law in this situation and shows instead that love and compassion are the best ways of responding to human failings. He does not tell the woman her adultery is morally acceptable –it's still a *sin* – but he refuses to punish her and gives her a second chance to sort her life out.

This is a very beautiful passage; possibly the most morally beautiful thing Jesus does during his Ministry. However, it has not been very influential on Christian ethics. The Early Churches did not forgive members who committed adultery and other sexual sins and modern churches tend to be far more condemning of sexual misbehaviour than things like being selfish with money (which Jesus has a *lot* more to say about).

*If you study **Unit 3 (New Testament Studies)**, you will come across the idea of a 'pericope' when you study **Form Criticism**. Scholars like **Bart Ehrman** argue that this passage was originally in a different source (perhaps Luke's Gospel), but Christians felt uncomfortable with its tolerant message; the story was inserted into John's Gospel by Christians who took a slightly more relaxed view of sexual sin. This suggests that the Law of Love has always been a rather challenging idea for people to come to terms with.*

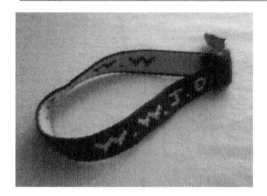

In the 1990s, Christian youth groups often wore wristbands with the motto **WWJD: What Would Jesus Do?**

The phrase helps to remind Christian believers to adopt a loving, compassionate perspective rather than acting selfishly or following popular customs and traditions. It makes them think twice rather than following the crowd. It acts as a reminder that there is always a better way to conduct ourselves.

*Note however that many of the churches who popularised **WWJD** in the '90s reject Fletcher's **Situationalism**, just as most Christian churches do not follow Jesus' example of forgiving people who commit adultery! Be careful about writing in the exam that WWJD is **the same thing** as Situation Ethics: SE focuses on Jesus enacting the Law of Love in his words and actions which is more radical than just 'trying to be a good Christian' in a conventional sense.*

SPECIFIC CASE STUDIES

Joseph Fletcher sets out four ideas about what Situation Ethics instructs us to do when we work out the right course of action:

- **Pragmatism:** Being pragmatic means asking yourself what is possible. Fletcher is saying that, if your moral system is telling you to do something that isn't possible or isn't bearable, then your moral system is flawed. This is particularly relevant to cases like abortion, where some moral systems (eg Catholic beliefs) might insist a mother goes through with a pregnancy even though it will damage or kill her.

- **Relativism:** The right thing to do depends on (*is relative to*) the situation. Relativism is a bit of a dirty word for some ethical thinkers who say we must stick to our principles come-what-may. Fletcher disagrees, saying a good moral system *'relativizes the absolute, it does not absolutize the relative'*. **Absolutism** (p7) is the idea that rules should never be broken, but Fletcher thinks absolutes like 'Do not steal' sometimes become relative – if love demands stealing food for the hungry, you steal, just like Jean Valjean in **Les Misérables** who goes to prison for stealing a loaf of bread to feed his family. It doesn't mean 'anything goes'. Fletcher still believes in sticking to moral rules in ordinary situations.

- **Positivism:** Natural Law and Utilitarianism are based on reason – reason can decide the right course of action, either from the purpose of life or the promotion of pleasure. Fletcher disagrees with this. He thinks a good moral system is based on the positive choice to love other people and to try to do good. If you make morality all about reason, your moral system will lead you to do evil or hurtful things; only a moral system based on positive *agápē* avoids this.

- **Personalism:** Fletcher believes in putting people first. People are more important than rules. Someone who puts laws and rules ahead of people is a **'legalist'** (p7) but Fletcher points out that Jesus said: *"The Sabbath was made for man, not man for the Sabbath"* (**Mark 2: 27**), meaning that it's more important to do right by other people than to follow rules legalistically.

Fletcher gives many examples to show the problems with ignoring his Four Working Principles when you make ethical decisions. He claims these true stories came from the people he met in his job as a priest. Fletcher is not saying he has the definite answers to these dilemmas. He is showing that neither **Utilitarianism** (p10) nor traditional **Deontology** (p6) solves these problems, and his Working Principles suggest a better approach.

> *These case studies are evaluated later from the perspective of **Natural Moral Law** (p57)*

Himself might his quietus make

> *I dropped in on a patient at the hospital who explained that he only had a set time to live. The doctors could give him some pills (that would cost $40 every three days) that would keep him alive for the next three years, but if he didn't take the pills, he'd be dead within six months. Now he was insured for $100,000, double indemnity and that was all the insurance he had. But if he took the pills and lived past next October when the insurance was up for renewal, they were bound to refuse the renewal, and his insurance would be cancelled. So he told me that he was thinking that if he didn't take the pills, then his family would get left with some security, and asked my advice on the situation* – **Joseph Fletcher**

> *The odd title of this case study is from* **Hamlet**, *in Hamlet's famous "To be or not to be" speech (Act III, scene i). Hamlet considers suicide (which is what 'quietus' means).*

The dying man is considering VOLUNTARY EUTHANASIA: if he stops taking his medication he will die and his family will get a big insurance payout; if he keeps taking the pills he will live a bit longer and his family gets nothing. Traditional morality (such as **Natural Moral Law**, p57) would say it is wrong to commit euthanasia because life is sacred. **Utilitarianism** (p10) would coldly weigh up one person's life and happiness as less important than the whole family's happiness. However, this would lead to the conclusion that all dying patients should receive euthanasia whether they want it or not.

Fletcher finds both responses lacking. The patient is motivated by love for his family: he wants to provide for them and not be a burden; he wants his death to have meaning and accomplish something. Fletcher seems to feel that a Christian could oppose euthanasia in most circumstances, but still recognise that *this* situation is different.

- **Pragmatism:** The patient has an opportunity to do something special for his family
- **Relativism:** In this particular situation, with the odd timing of his insurance policy being renewed, the patient's decision should be judged differently
- **Positivism:** The patient is motivated by love for his family: he wants them to be well provided for after he dies
- **Personalism:** We should put what this patient wants for himself and his family ahead of rules that go against his wishes

This situation shows a clear difference between traditional Christian ethics – especially Catholic ethics – and Fletcher's situationalism. The traditional Christian view would be that humans have no right to take their own life and have a duty to live as long as God intends them to. The correct response is humility and prayer, not arrogantly taking the power of life and death into your own hands, particularly when the motive is money.

Fletcher sees this as putting your principles before the needs of a person in distress. He thinks that Situationalism would permit the dying man to end his life early without approving of euthanasia in any and all situations.

Special Bombing Mission No. 13

*When the atomic bomb was dropped on Hiroshima, the plane crew were silent. Captain Lewis uttered six words, "My God, what have we done?" Three days later another one fell on Nagasaki. About 152,000 were killed; many times more were wounded and burned, to die later. The next day Japan sued for peace. When deciding whether to use "the most terrible weapon ever known" the US President appointed an Interim Committee made up of distinguished and responsible people in the government. Most but not all of its military advisors favoured using it. Top-level scientists said they could find no acceptable alternative to using it, but they were opposed by equally able scientists. After lengthy discussions, the committee decided that the lives saved by ending the war swiftly by using this weapon outweighed the lives destroyed by using it and thought that the best course of action – **Joseph Fletcher**

Atomic bombs have been used twice in history. The USA brought WWII to an end by dropping nuclear bombs on the Japanese cities of Hiroshima and Nagasaki in August 1945. It is still debated to this day whether these acts were war crimes.

This was an exceptional case: over 50 million people died in WWII; in the Pacific conflict with Japan, the Americans took nearly half a million casualties and the Japanese nearly 3 million in there battles with the Americans, the British and the Chinese. If Japan did not surrender, Operation Downfall was the plan for invading Japan from the sea: the Americans expected anything up to 4 million casualties and the Japanese casualties would have been 5-10 million. The country would have been devastated.

After Japan's surrender, the USA funded the rebuilding of the country along democratic lines, with $500 million a year in aid. Japan experienced an 'economic miracle' of productivity and wealth and is famous today for its successful car and technology industries.

Was atomic bombing the right thing to do?

- **Utilitarians** (p10) would say 'Yes' because the casualties of the two bombings were a fraction of what would have happened had the war continued: ending the war quickly minimized suffering.
- **Pacifists** (*c.f.* **Topic 3: War & Peace**) would say 'No' because the victims of the bombs were innocent civilians: targeting civilians in war is always wrong.

Fletcher seems to find both viewpoints flawed. The utilitarians lack a sense of moral horror at what was done (as shown by Cap. Lewis' six words) and we would not normally agree with winning wars by bombing civilians; the pacifists allow their principles to condemn millions of people to deaths that could be prevented.

Christian cloak & dagger

I was reading ... on a shuttle plane to New York. Next to me sat a young woman of about twenty-eight or so, attractive and well turned out in expensive clothes of good taste. She showed some interest in my book, and I asked if she'd like to look at it. "No", she said, "I'd rather talk ... I have a problem I'm confused about. You might help me to decide," she explained... There was a war going on that her government believed could be stopped by some clever use of espionage and blackmail. However, this meant she had to seduce and sleep with an enemy spy in order to lure him into blackmail. Now this went against her morals, but if it brought the war to an end, saving thousands of lives, would it be worth breaking those standards? – **Joseph Fletcher**

'Cloak & Dagger' is an old-fashioned term for what we call 'spy stories' these days: stuff like James Bond *where people go undercover and do secret plots.*

The female spy in this story is having a moral crisis. Her government wants her to take part in a 'honey trap' (using sex to manipulate or blackmail an enemy) but this goes against her moral standards (it might be an act of adultery if either she or the enemy spy is married and it is certainly using sex to trick and harm somebody rather than as an expression of love).

Once again, standard ethical theories are flawed in how they respond to this:

- **Utilitarianism** (p10) would easily conclude that happiness is maximized by carrying out the 'honey trap': thousands of lives will be saved in exchange for two people being hurt. There is a failure here to recognise the value of personal integrity and the moral horror of betrayal.
- Traditional deontological ethics (such as **Natural Moral Law**, p57) would say it is always wrong to have sex outside of marriage – and even liberals who accept non-marital sex would draw the line at sex used to exploit someone. There is a danger here of putting principles ahead of the common good.

Situationalism would suggest that the female spy's mission is **pragmatic** and must be judged **relativistically** (this is an exceptional situation). If the spy goes through with it, her choice is **positive** (she is doing it for her country) and **personal** (she can set her principles aside this one time).

On the other hand, SE might suggest the mission is ***not* pragmatic** (if the spy cannot bring herself to go through with it) and perhaps loyalty to country should be judged **relativistically** (with personal integrity counting for more than patriotism). Her choice ***not*** to go through with the mission could be **positive** (especially if she is considering her husband or the other spy's wife) and **personal** (it's more important to do the right thing for individual people than follow instructions from your leaders).

SE doesn't offer one-size fits all solutions to ethical problems. The woman in the story must work out for herself whether this mission is something she can go through with a still respect herself.

Sacrificial adultery

As the Russian armies drove westward to meet the Americans and British at the Elbe, a Soviet patrol picked up a Mrs Bergmeier foraging food for her three children. Unable even to get word to the children, she was taken off to a POW camp in Ukraine. Her husband had been captured in the Battle of the Bulge and taken to a POW camp in Wales. When he was returned to Berlin, he spent months rounding up his children, although they couldn't find their mother. She more than anything else was needed to reconnect them as a family in that dire situation of hunger, chaos and fear.

Meanwhile, in Ukraine, Mrs Bergmeier learned through a sympathetic commandant that her husband and family were trying to keep together and find her. But the rules allowed them to release her to Germany only if she was pregnant, in which case she would be returned as a liability. She turned things over in her mind and finally asked a friendly Volga German camp guard to impregnate her, which he did. Her condition being medically verified, she was sent back to Berlin and to her family. They welcomed her with open arms, even when she told them how she had managed it. And when the child was born, they all loved him because of what it had done for them. **– Joseph Fletcher**

This story is set during WWII when many people living in Eastern Europe found themselves caught between the Allies (British and American) and the Russians who were advancing on Berlin. Some families (like this one) got split up when they were taken to different POW camps (Mrs Bergmeier in the Ukraine, her husband in Wales).

This is the most famous of Fletcher's case studies. It is unusual because Fletcher tells us how it ends: the family is reunited and instead of being angry at his wife's infidelity Mr Bergmeier forgives her and accepts the child she carries as his own.

In a way, this case study follows on from **Christian Cloak & Dagger** (p41) because it concerns sexual infidelity. However, in this case there is nothing ambiguous about the situation: having sex with another man has wholly good consequences for her family; staying in the POW camp would have been disastrous for them.

It's important to understand that Mrs Bergmeier is not motivated by **romantic/erotic love** (where she is so desperate to be reunited with her husband she will sleep with another man to win her heart's desire); rather, she is motivated by *agápē* (she knows her husband and children cannot cope without her and wishes to be reunited so she can help them).

This case study goes to the heart of Christian teachings about sex:

- Adultery is condemned by the **7th Commandment**
- Sex is not to be used as an **instrument** for accomplishing things: it is for **expressing love** and **conceiving children within a marriage**

However, Fletcher implies that Mrs Bergmeier acts selflessly here, according to the Law of Love, even though she has broken her marriage vows and gone against Christian teachings. Fletcher claims: *"Sex is not always wrong outside marriage, even for Christians."*

EVALUATING SITUATIONALISM

Situation Ethics is a very appealing approach. It avoids the written-in-stone rigidity of traditional ethics and the rather judgmental, heartless positions that **Deontology** (p6) can take on many subjects. It has the flexibility of **Utilitarianism** (p10), without the strange, perverse conclusions that utilitarians can arrive at. It seems to embody some of the most striking and attractive features of Jesus' thinking about ethics. It also seems well-suited to resolving many of the ethical dilemmas facing ordinary people in the 21st century: abortion and divorce, racism and sexism, multiculturalism, etc.

Situation Ethics is sensitive to circumstances, context and cultural traditions. Every moral decision is required to show respect for individuals and communities (**personalism**) and the things that they regard as valuable (**relativism**). This avoids the logical, detached and impersonal ways of thinking that other ethical systems tend to emphasize (**positivism**). Because moral decisions are treated on a case-by-case basis, the decision is always tailored to particular situations (**pragmatism**).

Situation Ethics claims to be the solution to two problematic tendencies in ethics – the tendency towards rule-bound ethics (**legalism**) and no rules at all (**antinomianism**). It has one rule: love. It is simple and yet profound. It is not meant to encourage laxity. It calls for **self-giving, unconditional willing of another's good** – *agápē*, not just "niceness" or "decency". It aims to skirt the problems arising when a situation brings important rules into conflict. It simply says: 'Do the most loving thing.' Fletcher describes cases when the moral rules do not address the real problem.

On the other hand, Situationalism has a similar problem to **Utilitarianism** – it depends on the individual's appraisal of situations. A person, even with the best of intentions, cannot foresee every consequence of an action, nor how many people likely to be affected by it. What if **Mrs Bergmeier's husband** (p42) had been shocked at her infidelity and abandoned her and the baby? What if the guard who fathered the baby demanded his child to raise as his own? A Christian might have faith that, so long as they act on *agápē*, God will not allow anything to go wrong. But this sort of faith can't be the basis of an ethical system **everyone** is supposed to follow, since plainly bad things happen sometimes despite good intentions.

Even this assumes that a person's decision-making isn't distorted by selfishness or laziness. Many people don't *want* to aim for the high standards of *agápē*. A more rule-dependent moral system would be helpful for ordinary people and protect others from selfishness disguising itself as 'love'. For example, a man cheating on his wife could persuade himself that he's really doing the 'loving' thing if he comes home to his wife with gifts and takes her on romantic holidays. The Seventh Commandment (**Exodus 20: 14**) is very clear: adultery is always wrong, even if you 'make up for it' by treating your partner kindly!

Situation Ethics might approve of 'evil' acts. You might think this is surprising, since SE is supposed to follow the Law of Love, but SE teaches that particular types of action don't have an **intrinsic** moral value – whether they are good or bad depends on the motive and eventual result.

The **Ticking Time Bomb Dilemma** asks you to choose between torturing a captured terrorist to learn the location of a bomb, or refusing to use torture at the risk of allowing the bomb to go off, killing innocent people.

Some types of **Utilitarianism** would approve of torture since it maximizes happiness, but **Natural Moral Law** would claim that torture is always wrong and cannot be justified. Despite this, in the Middle Ages, the monks and priests working for the Inquisition tortured many people "for the good of their souls". Would someone following Situation Ethics become a torturer too in the right situation?

Peter Vardy accuses SE as being no different from Utilitarianism in practice:

> [Situation Ethics] *is almost identical to utilitarianism except that 'love' has been substituted for 'happiness'* – **Peter Vardy**

Critics say that, despite all the messages in the Bible, it's not really clear what *agápē* means. Although the notion of **selfless love** used in SE seems attractive, it's pretty vague and can be interpreted in many ways. For example, does 'loving' someone mean *sparing* them suffering or comforting them *during* their suffering? This makes a big difference if a sick relative is asking you to help them carry out euthanasia. It seems strange if one person can 'love' their grandfather by administering fatal drug overdose while another person 'loves' their grandmother by caring for them through years of sickness. If both of these acts are 'love' then it's tempting to conclude that we need a better word (or maybe, like the Ancient Greeks, several different words).

Changes to Law & Social Attitudes

Critics have pointed out that Situation Ethics does away with talk about universal moral truths and seems to remove any possibility of guaranteeing HUMAN RIGHTS. This makes it very hard to use SE in politics or court cases and almost impossible to apply it to international law.

For example, in the 1980s many countries boycotted products from the apartheid regime in South Africa because of the unjust way it treated the black population. Where would SE stand on this? Does *agápē* demand that you buy South African oranges in order to make sure poor black farm workers get paid? Or should you boycott the products and bring down an evil regime, even if that means poverty for the farm workers? **Natural Moral Law** (p57) with its emphasis on human rights or **Utilitarianism** (p10) with its focus on maximizing happiness might help settle this dilemma, but SE doesn't have a clear answer.

The Law of Love is often summed up in the popular phrase "*What Would Jesus Do?* However, during the war in Afghanistan and Iraq in the 2000s, US President **George W. Bush** told reporters: "*I am doing what Jesus would have done*". This shows one of the flaws with Situation Ethics and WWJD when it comes to making big decisions like going to war – SE can justify *any* course of action. If WWJD justifies declaring war, we might wonder what *wouldn't* Jesus do?

Despite these reservations, SE has been influential in America and Britain, especially in laws surrounding relationships.

- Before the **Divorce Reform Act 1969**, most people married for life and divorce was only available if you could prove your partner was unfaithful and cruel. Since 1970, couples can get divorces if the marriage is 'irretrievably broken down' (i.e. living apart for 2 years, 5 years if one of them still wants to remain married). This no longer traps people in loveless and abusive marriages.

- Further changes are coming after the **Tini Owens Case (2018)** where a woman unhappily married for 40 years wanted a divorce without having to wait another 5 years. Her petition failed, but many people felt the law was unfair and the Government has promised to bring forward 'No Fault Divorces' so that couples will be able to get divorced without these restrictions.

- The **Marriage (Same Sex Couples) Act 2013** legalised marriages for same-sex couples, replacing the earlier Civil Partnerships. This reflects a big shift of opinion in British society: a 2012 poll found 71% of the British public supported same-sex marriage (**source: YouGov**), compared to the 1980s when a similar proportion regarded homosexuality as 'always wrong'

The introduction of laws against 'Hate Crimes' reflect society's distaste for cruelty and bullying; the law tries to show compassion and care towards people in need

Compatibility with religious approaches

Joseph Fletcher (p78) and **J.A.T. Robinson** (p81) both argue that agapeic ethics represents the very essence of Christian thinking about goodness and the heart of Jesus' message about how to live. They see themselves as recovering an insight that was lost during centuries of misguided **deontological** thinking. *Agápē* is the piece of the puzzle that completes Christian ethics and makes sense of Jesus' teachings.

For example, **St Paul** wrote that *"love is the fulfilment of the law"* (**Romans 13: 10**). This suggests that *agápē* and moral laws need each other. Love needs law for its direction, while law needs love for its inspiration. I

When someone acts lovingly, there are certain things they will ***always*** do and certain things they will ***never*** do. Deontological rules, like the **Ten Commandments**, could be what Fletcher calls *'crystallisations of love'*: they represent how a loving person will behave ***most of the time***. But there are exceptions and *agápē* is the best guide to when these exceptions occur and what should be done when they happen.

However, religious believers have been critical of Situationalism. Jesus states that there are ultimately two commandments that matter: loving God and loving your neighbour (**Matthew 22: 36-40**). SE focuses entirely on loving your neighbour but it seems to downplay loving God, since it encourages going against God's commands.

45

For example, SE claims to be based on the statement "*God is Love*" (**I John 4:8**) – therefore, anything done out of love must please God. However, in the next chapter of the same New Testament book, the author says:

> *This is love for God: to keep his commands. And his commands are not burdensome –* **1 John 5: 3**

Fletcher believes that any of God's commands may be broken if Love is the intention. This is why he thinks: "*Sex is not always wrong outside marriage, even for Christians.*" Traditional Christians point out that keeping God's commands *is* loving God. This means breaking the command about, say, not committing adultery cannot be done out of *agápē*.

Situation Ethics also makes the assumption that ordinary humans are capable for acting out of *agápē* in a consistent and unbiased way. This is doubtful even from the viewpoint of ordinary psychology: we lack self-knowledge about our own true feelings and motives, so we fool ourselves into thinking we are acting out of love when really we are not.

Traditional Christians would go further than this, because they believe humans are Fallen creatures who are sinful by nature (Catholics refer to this as ORIGINAL SIN). Trying to make *agápē* the basis of our ethical thinking is crediting us with more goodness than we really possess. **J.A.T. Robinson** thinks that SE is the only ethical theory for "*man come of age*" (p81), but traditional Christians would deny that man has come of age, or will ever come of age, until Judgement Day arrives. Despite all their science and progress, humans in the 21st century are as sinful as they've ever been.

The Catholic Church had already condemned Situation Ethics before Fletcher or Robinson wrote their books. **Pope Pius XII (1952)** warned Christians not to listen to people who called for softening Christian rules on response to the New Morality. The Catholic Church retains its commitment to **Natural Moral Law** (p57) and a **deontological** view of right and wrong.

However, the current **Pope Francis** might be an exception. He frequently attacks "*rigidity*" in Catholic ethics and his recent sermon **Amoris Laetitia (2016)** argues that a person can be in **a situation where they have no choice but to sin**. The Pope is offering support to Catholic homosexuals by acknowledging that they cannot help feeling the way they do, but critics claim he is doing so by embracing ethical theories like Situationalism or **Proportionalism** (p68) which were rejected by previous Popes.

ANTHOLOGY EXTRACT #1

There are 4 Anthology extracts for A-Level Religion & Ethics: this one features in Year 1 and the other 3 feature in Year 2. AS-Level students will benefit from reading this extract too because it summarises **Joseph Fletcher's Situation Ethics** and offers thoughtful criticisms.

The author, **William Barclay (1907-1978**, *right***)**, was a Church of Scotland minister. Barclay's views are rather contradictory. He describes himself as a *"liberal evangelical"* (the two terms are usually opposed, since liberals reject a strict Christian theology and evangelicals tend to take the Bible literally).

- Barclay is a **liberal** because he is a pacifist, a universalist (he does not believe in Hell and thinks all human souls go to Heaven) and he denies the Virgin Birth and other miracles.
- He is an **evangelical** because he believes in Jesus' literal Resurrection and argues that the Gospels are eyewitness accounts rather than documents composed much later in history.

In 1971, Barclay delivered the Baird Lecture on BBC TV with the title *Jesus Today: the Christian Ethic in the Twentieth Century*. The TV lecture was such a success that it was published as a book, ***Ethics in a Permissive Society* (1971)**. Chapter 4 from this book forms the extract.

You can read the entire book on the Baird Trust website:
http://www.clydeserver.com/bairdtrust/

Ethics in a Permissive Society (William Barclay, 1971)

Barclay begins by considering **deontology** in ethics (p6), which is the traditional view:

> *Mostly we take it that ethics classifies words and actions into things which are good and things which are bad, and we take it that the goodness and the badness belong to the thing as such.*

He doesn't mention deontology by name, but the idea that the moral character of an act *"belongs to the thing as such"* rather than being found in its consequences is the definition of deontology.

Barclay goes on to introduce **Joseph Fletcher's Situation Ethics** (or **Situationalism**):

> *Fletcher's basic principle is that there is nothing which is universally right or universally wrong; there is nothing which is intrinsically good or intrinsically bad. Goodness and badness are not built in, essential, unchangeable qualities of anything*

This is a good analysis of SE and its contrast with **deontology**. Barclay talks about things which are *"universally"* or *"unchangeably"* or *"intrinsically"* good or bad. This is a deontological view: bad things are wrong for everyone (*universal*), all the time (*unchangeable*) and they are wrong just for being what they are rather than because of their consequences (*intrinsic*). SE denies that things are like this. **Nothing** is wrong for everybody, all the time, just because of what it is.

Barclay sums up how Situationalists view moral principles:

> *Principles are only tools in the hand of God, soon to be thrown away as unserviceable*

He suggests that Situationalists only treat moral principles as temporary guidelines rather than permanent rules. His language is perhaps a bit extreme. **Joseph Fletcher** regards moral principles as *"the crystallization of love"* and certainly doesn't think they should be *"thrown away"* – just occasionally set to one side when the need arises.

Barclay presents Situationalists as people who *"completely refuse to be shackled or bound by anything."* Fletcher would regard this as ANTINOMIANISM (the rejection of any sort of moral law) and reply that SE is supposed to be a middle-way between **antinomianism and legalism** (p7).

Setting out a falsely exaggerated version of your opponent's views is a STRAW MAN ARGUMENT (because knocking down a straw man – like a scarecrow – is easy but doesn't prove anything about how strong you are). Since Barclay confuses Situationalism with antinomianism, he could be accused of making a 'straw man' argument.

The Meaning of 'Love'

Barclay goes on to analyse the meaning of love. He contrasts the four words for 'love' in Ancient Greek:

- **ERŌS**: This is similar to the ordinary use of 'love' in English since it means romantic or sexual love, usually between a couple. *Erōs* is a passionate love: you can't make it start or make it stop just with willpower and you often feel it towards people who don't deserve it – or fail to feel it towards people who do.
- **PHILIA**: This is 'brotherly love' or friendship-love. It involves *"loyalty and companionship"* and often shared interests. To an extent, you can choose your friends, which is unlike the passion of *erōs*. However, you only tend to feel *philia* for people who are like you in some way or who share your pastimes.
- **STORGĒ**: This is family love. You don't choose your family, so in a way this is more like *erōs* than *philia*. However, it's not passionate and definitely not sexual. You don't even have to **like** your family members very much in order to feel this tie to them (the Greeks also used this word for loving your pets or even objects of sentimental value).
- **AGÁPĒ**: This is selfless, compassionate love. Barclay calls it *"unconquerable goodwill"* and *"the determination always to seek the other man's highest good, no matter what he does to you."* Unlike *erōs*, it has nothing to do with sex or passion; unlike *philia*, it isn't based on people's deserts or how nice they are; unlike *storgē* you can express it towards people who are completely unconnected to you.

It's important to remember that the English language uses the same word, 'love', for all four types. This can lead to confusion. A person can justify adultery because they 'love' someone, but this love is *erōs*, which is nothing to do with *agápē*.

C.S. Lewis (1958) calls *agápē* the highest of the four loves and Barclay agrees. The appeal of *agápē* in ethics is that this sort of love is a ***choice*** not a ***feeling***. This is why *"we can love the person we don't like."* However, the question is, Can you build an ethical system on *agápē*?

Some Thought-Experiments

Barclay offers a set of thought-experiments (like **Fletcher's case studies**, p38) to test out how *agápē* works as an ethical guide. The first is simple:

> *A house catches fire and in it there is a baby and the original of the Mona Lisa; which do you save the baby or the priceless and irreplaceable picture?*

Traditional ethics would say 'the baby' and so would SE, because this is showing *agápē*. However, Barclay offers another **burning house thought-experiment** that is less clear-cut:

> *Suppose in the burning house there is your aged father, an old man, with the days of his usefulness at an end, and a doctor who has discovered a cure for one of the world's great killer diseases, and who still carries the formulae in his head, and you can save only one – whom do you save?*

A **utilitarian** (p10) would save the doctor because his cure will help lots of people; traditional ethics would say we have a duty towards our parents (*"honour your father and mother"* is the Fifth Commandment) and this is in line with most people's gut feelings. What would a Situationalist do? Your love for your father is *storgē*, not *agápē*, but it doesn't ***feel*** like the more loving thing to leave your ageing father to die in order to rescue a stranger, no matter how socially valuable that stranger is. If SE tells us to ignore family-love, then it seems to be urging us to do the same rather cold, perverse things that Utilitarianism urges us to do.

Barclay offers another, even more troubling thought-experiment. This one involves the American pioneer **Daniel Boone (1734-1820**, *right*). In 1775, Boone scouted the 'Wilderness Road' through the Appalachian Mountains, enabling brave settlers to create the state of Kentucky. This was a dangerous journey, due to hostile Native American tribes who would (perhaps understandably) attack the settlers moving into their lands.

Barclay narrates two incidents where the settlers had to hide from the Natives. In one case, a baby's cries gave the settlers away *"and the party was discovered and all were massacred."* On a different occasion, a mother strangled her baby to stop it crying: she saved all the settlers by sacrificing her child. Barclay asks: *"Which action was love?"*

> *Barclay wrote this in the 1970s and was a man in his 60s at the time: he uses dated terms. "Indian" is still a common (but politically incorrect) term for Native American; "Negro" is no longer an acceptable term for African-American, but it would not have had racist connotations for Barclay. Nonetheless, you might prefer to use the modern terms in the exam if you write about this incident.*

This is another confusing dilemma. The mother's love for her child is also *storgē*, not *agápē*, but it does not seem ethical that children be sacrificed, even if murdering them saves the lives of many adults. A **utilitarian** would support strangling the child – but this would often be a criticism of Utilitarianism that it fails to recognise SPECIAL DUTIES towards innocent children.

Barclay doesn't offer any ideas about what the correct answer is: he just leaves us with the growing impression that acting upon *agápē* is not as straightforward as you might think.

Barclay sums up the Situationalist viewpoint quite accurately:

> *There are principles, of course, but they can only advise; they do not have the right of veto. Any principle must be abandoned, left, disregarded, if the command to love your neighbour can be better served by so doing.*

He illustrates this with Fletcher's anecdote about the St Louis cab driver telling a passenger *"there are times when a man has to push his principles aside, and do the right thing!"*

It's significant that the 'principles' in this story aren't really moral principles (like not stealing or lying) but political loyalties. The cab driver is going to vote Democrat rather than Republican despite being a lifelong Republican. There might be moral reasons behind this (maybe the Republican candidate is corrupt or maybe an issue like abortion or civil rights is involved). A critic might argue that, in a healthy democracy, voters are **supposed** to change sides in special situations rather than mindlessly voting for the same party again and again. So perhaps this anecdote doesn't really support the idea of abandoning moral principles.

The Rainmaker

Barclay gives a fictional example of moral principles being *"set aside"*: **N. Richard Nash**'s play ***The Rainmaker* (1954)**, which was made into a 1956 movie with Hollywood legends Burt Lancaster and Katherine Hepburn. In the play, Lizzie Curry is an unmarried woman (a 'spinster') with a failing farm who is desperate to marry the local sheriff. A charming conman named Starbuck arrives, promising he can make the drought end and save the farm.

> *The Rainmaker is a romantic comedy – you can watch it on YouTube (search for "1956 Full Movie"). It was still quite famous when Fletcher was writing in the '60s.*

Fletcher uses the play as an example and Barclay summarises a key scene, where Starbuck *"makes love"* to Lizzie in the barn and Lizzie's father defends him, saying to Lizzie's indignant brother: *"You're so full of what's right that you can't see what's good."*

The play doesn't reveal what goes on in the barn after Starbuck and Lizzie kiss, but audiences assume they share a 'one night stand' and this is positive for Lizzie: Starbuck makes her see herself as beautiful and she goes on to stand up for herself and win over the sheriff.

The idea of a casual sexual encounter being psychologically healthy is part of the **New Morality** (p31) which celebrates pleasure and shedding inhibitions, but it goes against traditional ethics which regards such behaviour as FORNICATION. The play suggests that this encounter isn't *"right"* (in terms of traditional ethics) but it's still *"good"* (in terms of the New Morality).

But of course *The Rainmaker* is fiction and has an unlikely happy ending: Lizzie ends up with the sheriff and the rains arrive as if by magic. In real life, casual sex often has bad effects: anxiety, shame, low self-esteem and, of course, unwanted pregnancy and STIs. All of these real-life issues are ignored in Nash's fairytale ending.

Justice & Love

Barclay moves on to discuss the issue of 'justice' and whether Situation Ethics can help solve injustice in the world. He considers criticisms by two other philosophers:

- **Reinhold Niebuhr (1892–1971)** is an American Christian thinker who supported social justice (especially working class causes) but who opposed **relativism in ethics** (p7). Barclay quotes Niebuhr as saying: *"love is transcendent and love is impossible; while justice is something by which we can live in this present society."* In other words, love is an ideal but justice is something different that we can and should work towards.
- **Emil Brunner (1889-1996)** is a Swiss Christian thinker who opposed liberalism in Christianity. Barclay quotes Brunner as saying: *"love must be between two persons; whereas justice exists between groups."* This is another reason why *agápē* cannot solve problems in society, which usually involve groups not individual persons.

Barclay then examines Fletcher's idea that *"justice is love distributed."* Barclay finds this an appealing idea. He gives the example of the famous entertainer **Sammy Davis Jr** (*right*) who was wildly popular as a singer, actor and comedian in the 1950s and '60s but suffered discrimination as a black man in America. He converted to Judaism because he felt drawn to the Jewish idea of justice and had found the Christian idea of love to be rather hollow.

Barclay has sympathy with this view, but agrees that it doesn't count against Situationalism because *agápē* isn't just a **feeling**, it's a **decision** to act a certain way towards other people.

Love has always got to be thinking; love has always got to be calculating

The Bible supports this idea of *agápē* as *"thinking"* and *"calculating"* when Jesus advises his followers to be *"as wise as serpents but as innocent as doves"* (**Matthew 10: 16**).

Barclay seems to end up supporting this view of justice as *"love working out its problems"* – which goes to show he doesn't criticise **all** of Fletcher's ideas.

Sacrificial Adultery

Barclay next considers Fletcher's famous **case study of Mrs Bergmeier** (p42) who chooses to become pregnant by another man so that she can reunite her family.

As with the other examples, Barclay doesn't make his own view clear at first but asks the reader to reflect: *"Right or wrong? Adultery or love? Which?"*

Barclay offers a criticism of Fletcher's case studies as a whole:

> *Fletcher's illustrations are drawn from the abnormal, the unusual and the extraordinary*

Mrs Bergmeier is an exceptional and unusual story: most cases of adultery aren't like *that*. Similarly, **The Rainmaker** is a fictional story with a fairytale ending: real life one-night stands don't end like *that* either. **Daniel Boone's settlers**, faced with strangling a baby, are also in a very abnormal situation that never happens to most people, even in the 18th century American Frontier.

Barclay questions whether these bizarre scenarios justify creating a whole new ethical theory:

> *It is much easier to agree that extraordinary situations need extraordinary measures than to think that there are no laws for ordinary everyday life.*

However, Barclay admits that this criticism is *"not so much of situation ethics as it is of Fletcher's presentation of it"* – in other words, it's a criticism of Fletcher's unusual examples but not of Fletcher's underlying point, that morality should be about putting *agápē* into action.

Moreover, Fletcher would be the first to admit that, in *"ordinary, everyday life,"* the old-fashioned moral principles and rules apply most of the time. The question is, when *are* we in an *"extraordinary situation"* that justifies abandoning those principles? Trying to answer this leads on to Barclay's most serious criticism of Situationalism.

"A Terrifying Degree of Freedom"

Barclay points out that, if we follow Situation Ethics, we are constantly in the position of having to work out whether to stick with traditional principles or abandon them – and we can never know for sure if we have made the right choice.

To a degree, Barclay accepts this as inevitable. He cites **Emil Brunner** (p51) who points out that, for Christians, there is *"nowhere you can go – not even to the Sermon on the Mount and say: 'Now I know what to do.' There is no such thing as a readymade decision."*

The **Sermon on the Mount (Matthew 5-7)** is a passage where Jesus explains his ethical ideas, notably **loving your enemies**, putting aside **material concerns** and **not judging others**. It is considered the highpoint of Christian ethical thought. However, as Brunner recognises, it doesn't cover *every* situation. So even if we reject Situationalism, we will still find ourselves in situations at times where traditional ethical rules don't tell us exactly what to do.

However, Barclay thinks Situation Ethics goes much further than Brunner's point that we sometimes find ourselves in unfamiliar ethical situations where it's not clear what's best. Barclay claims that Situationalists have "*a kind of phobia of law*": they are opposed to the idea that there are **ever** rules that you simply have to follow.

Is this a fair criticism? Fletcher rejects **antinomianism** (p7) which is the idea that there are simply no moral rules at all. Barclay seems to think the Situationalism is a sort of SLIPPERY SLOPE into antinomianism: once you start abandoning a few principles, you end up ditching all of them.

This slippery-slope argument isn't logically true of SE, but it might be psychologically true. Barclay thinks "*we need a certain amount of law, being the kind of people we are.*"

This boils down to two opposing views of human nature:

- Fletcher has an **optimistic** view, that human beings will figure out when to follow moral rules and will work out when to set them aside, because *agápē* is fairly easy to grasp
- Barclay has a **pessimistic** view, that human beings tend to be self-centred and biased in their thinking and that, once they abandon moral rules, they easily get confused about what *agápē* is (and perhaps confuse it with lesser types of love such as **erōs** and **storgē**, p48).

> *If all men were saints, then situation ethics would be the perfect ethics. John A. T. Robinson has called situation ethics 'the only ethic for man come of age'. This is probably true – but man has not yet come of age.*

Barclay references another situationalist, **J.A.T. Robinson** (p81) and his famous quote about "*man come of age.*" Barclay disagrees with Robinson that the human race has evolved past the need for rules and principles in ethics. He thinks we are not yet ready for that sort of moral freedom (and perhaps never will be).

Barclay's Views

Barclay (finally!) states his own views. He is a **deontologist** because he thinks "*there are things which can in no circumstances be right.*" He gives two examples:

- **DRUGS:** Experimenting with drugs can produce pleasant and even life-changing experiences, but the risks are so great that it can never be morally right to offer drugs to someone else.
- **ADULTERY/DIVORCE:** Breaking up a family is so harmful that it cannot be justified by appealing to love (either for someone else or what's 'best for the kids')

> *You might disagree with Barclay. He was writing only a year after the **Divorce Reform Act** had come into law and probably never suspected how widespread recreational drugs would become in the 21ˢᵗ century. Is he 'a man of his time' here or is he making a wise warning about behaviour which should not be accepted in society?*

Barclay offers two major criticisms of Situation Ethics from his Christian perspective: **Sublimation** and **God's Grace**.

Sublimation means transforming negative urges into positive behaviour. If your moral code forbids you from doing something violent or sexual, you could sublimate these urges into hard work or great art or scientific breakthroughs.

Barclay gives the example of the 18th century preacher **John Wesley** who founded the Methodist Church, but might not have accomplished so much good had he been happily married (Wesley's first love married another man and his later wife left him – several times!).

Sigmund Freud, a key influence on the **New Morality** (p31), developed the idea of sublimation in Psychology and offered the example of the artist **Leonardo Da Vinci**. Freud speculated that Leonardo was homosexual but, unable to express his feelings in 15th century Italy, he devoted himself to art instead.

Both of these examples make the point that sometimes more good can come out of denying yourself. However, Situation Ethics encourages people to think they don't need to deny themselves because they can set aside their principles instead.

However, this might be another of Barclay's STRAW MAN ARGUMENTS (*c.f.* p48). Situationalists will still find themselves in circumstances where they have to deny their desires. Situationalism is not the same as **antinomianism** (p7).

On the other hand, it's fair to say that Situationalists will end up denying their desires *much less often* than people who follow traditional ethics, especially as it's quite easy to justify abandoning your principles for the sake of love.

Grace of God refers to the way God intervenes in a person's life, perhaps through a **religious experience** (*c.f.* **Unit 1 Philosophy & Religion**) or answered prayers. In the Bible, Jesus says:

With God, all things are possible – **Matthew 19: 26**

Sometimes, the desire to abandon a moral principle is a temptation to be resisted:

- If **Mrs Bergmeier** had stayed faithful to her husband, she might have been freed without any need for adultery
- If the **mother on the Wilderness Trail** had not strangled her baby, the Native tribe might still have passed by without discovering the settlers – or even showed mercy to them

Situation Ethics can be seen as an attempt to 'play God' and bring about the loving outcome you assume God wants, but without waiting for God to do it in his own time – and at the cost of breaking God's commands. This makes SE the *opposite* of faith in God (and it's maybe no coincidence that Joseph Fletcher became an atheist in 1970, though Barclay was probably unaware of this).

Situation Ethics & the Law

Barclay concludes by moving away from moral laws to consider criminal laws. He explains the distinction between *crimes*, which are against the law and a matter of public concern, and *sins*, that are not against the law and are private matters. Barclay uses the example of the **Sexual Offences Act (1967)** which followed the recommendation of the **Wolfenden Report** and made homosexuality legal if it was in private between consenting adults.

> *In this section, the extract has a typo. The WOLFENDEN REPORT (with a F, not* **Wolenden***) was a committee led by Sir John Wolfenden that reported in 1957 that the UK should change the law to legalise homosexuality between consenting adults.*

Barclay calls this a distinction between **public crimes** and **private sins**: it is based on **J.S. Mill's Harm Principle (**p80**)** and is a cornerstone of political and ethical liberalism. Whatever you do in private, so long as no one is hurt and everyone consents, should be no business of the law.

However, Barclay thinks the Harm Principle leads to three *"tensions"* (contradictions or confusions) that Situation Ethics does not have an answer for.

1. **Freedom vs Law:** Situationalists value freedom highly. Barclay quotes **Joseph Fletcher** saying: *"Nothing we do is truly moral unless we are free to do otherwise . . . Morality is meaningless apart from freedom."* This idea of moral behaviour as *free* behaviour ties in with the Situationalist distrust of moral laws, but Barclay argues we are never really free in this way: we are restricted by the laws of the country, the customs of our community, our own upbringing and even our own biology. Barclay concludes the sort of freedom that Situationalists value is *"an illusion."*

2. **Immorality vs Illegality:** Situationalists value the Harm Principle but Barclay sees problems here. He mentions that one legal expert, **Lord Devlin**, argued against the Wolfenden Report that society ***should*** make things crimes because they are immoral, even if they don't hurt anyone. Barclay himself is concerned that *"what the law permits, it approves."* In other words, when you legalise something you encourage people to go out and do it.

> *Barclay gives examples that are so out-of-date they are almost comical (legalising homosexuality, allowing divorce, treating unmarried parents the same as married ones). Remember that Barclay was a bit out of touch even in 1971. However, modern examples can make the same point: decriminalising drugs tempts young people to try them; allowing gambling encourages people to get addicted; the availability of pornography promotes violence towards women.*

3. **Individual vs Community:** Barclay considers that Christianity and Judaism began in societies that did not encourage individualism, but modern society is intensely individualistic and Situation Ethics is part of this movement towards great individualism. Barclay warns that this trend can go too far and that *"it can never be right to develop [yourself] at the expense of others."* His point seems to be that Situationalism pushes us towards more individualism, but in fact we need to be pulled back the other way.

Barclay concludes by stating the problems he thinks a good ethical theory needs to solve:

> *One of the great problems of the present situation is to adjust the delicate balance between freedom and law, and between the individual and society.*

He seems to think that Situation Ethics is part of the problem and not part of the solution because it focuses too much on freedom, individualism and liberalism. However, his final sentence seems more positive towards SE:

> *And the only solution is that a man should discover what it means to love his neighbour as himself.*

Barclay clearly thinks there's something admirable and good in Situation Ethics and its focus on *agápē*. He thinks that any solution to our moral problems has to involve more *agápē*, not less. However, he is unconvinced that SE, in its current state, is the answer.

Evaluating *Ethics in a Permissive Society*

Earlier in his book, Barclay sums up Christian ethics like this:

> *The basis of the Christian ethic is concern* – **Ethics in a Permissive Society, chapter 2**

Barclay means compassionate concern for other people – in other words, *agápē*. Because he thinks this, Barclay has to be sympathetic towards Situation Ethics. He spends the first half of this extract exploring **Joseph Fletcher**'s ideas without much negative comment. In fact, he's very positive about Fletcher's idea that *"justice is love distributed."* He is in agreement with **Sammy Davis Jr**'s criticism that Christian love has, in the past, not done enough to combat racism. He's impressed by the insight that *"love has always got to be thinking; love has always got to be calculating"* which shows how *agápē* is different from just having nice **feelings** about people.

However, he cannot bring himself to agree with Fletcher because he is, at heart, a **deontologist** and believes that *"there are things which can in no circumstances be right."*

Barclay makes a number of criticisms of SE that are perhaps STRAW MAN ARGUMENTS. He frequently represents Situationalists as being **antinomians** who have a *"phobia of law"* and who *"refuse to be shackled or bound by anything."* He criticises Fletcher's case studies for being *"drawn from the abnormal, the unusual and the extraordinary"* but he admits this last point is not a criticism of the fundamental idea of *agápē* as the basis of ethics.

Barclay's more serious criticism is that SE is an ethical system for *"saints"* because *"man has not yet come of age."* SE puts people in a difficult situation of always having to work out whether to follow their principles or set them aside. Barclay thinks this is *"a terrifying degree of freedom"* and he thinks it is too hard for individuals to live this way and too destructive for society if this sort of individualism is encouraged.

Barclay seems rather regretful. He admires *agápē* as an ideal; he just regards it as impractical. However, he concludes by looking forward to a time when *"man should discover what it means to love his neighbour as himself."*

TOPIC 2.3 NATURAL MORAL LAW

There is another, older **deontological approach** (p6) to ethics which is still very influential today. The idea of a NATURAL MORAL LAW lies behind many religions, was first expounded by **Aristotle**, and forms the basis of modern notions of human rights. It was famously developed by **Thomas Aquinas** (p76) and it provides the ethical system favoured by the Catholic Church today.

The key assumption of Natural Moral Law (NML) is that there **is a moral code that humans are naturally inclined towards**. This means that, if people behave 'naturally' then they will be good. Being evil is 'unnatural.' Ordinary people often talk this way, particularly when they hear about shocking crimes and describe the offender as 'bestial' or 'monstrous.'

This is all well and good, but what exactly is 'natural behaviour' for human beings?

Foundations of the approach

Natural life is a life that completes and fulfils human beings: it is a happy life. The Greek word for happiness is *EUDAIMONIA*, so NML is a **eudaimonic ethical theory**.

However, *eudaimonia* is different from the pleasure/happiness that **Utilitarianism** promotes (p10). *Eudaimonia* is translated as "human flourishing and welfare" and it is a wider concept than simply having positive feelings. It's more about having a certain sort of **lifestyle**: one that is happy, but also healthy, productive and involves using your talents to their full. A person with a *eudaimon* life might be sad from time to time, but even while they are being unhappy, their life will still possess this positive quality, whereas a drug addict might experience a lot of (drug-induced) happiness, but never really knows *eudaimonia*.

Classical foundations

Aristotle (384-322 BCE) was perhaps the greatest philosopher in Ancient Greece and began the debate about *eudaimonia*, which he defines as *"living and doing well."* Aristotle argues that there is a certain sort of personality which has *eudaimon*: a virtuous personality that has been trained from an early age to like the right things and dislike bad things. The Greek word for this virtuous personality is ARETĒ (*ah-ret-tay*, which means something like 'excellence').

> *If you are an A-Level student, you will come across* **aretē** *again in Year 2 when you study* **Virtue Ethics** *in* **Topic 5**.

Education is vital for building a personality with *aretē* and there's no chance of holding on to *eudaimon* without having the right personality. This might strike you as odd: isn't *eudaimonia* about doing what comes naturally?

Aristotle argues that humans are RATIONAL ANIMALS: we are most human when we behave rationally. However, rationality is something we have to learn, just like young birds learn to fly. A human who is badly brought up will grow into someone who lives an irrational life, chasing after pleasure or status or new experiences but never having any sort of order in their life.

This means that children have to be taught to like the right things at an early age. At first they will keep promises, tell the truth, read Shakespeare and go to church because they are being made to; later in life, they will come to see the value in these things for themselves.

Aristotle praises a life of self-restraint and social responsibility. Not very exciting. Aristotle also doesn't look any further than his own society for the definition of the good (natural) life, so he cheerfully accepts slavery and the subordination of women on the grounds that some people (slaves, women) are 'naturally' less rational than free men. This flaw in NML – that it is very conservative and rarely challenges social roles or the wisdom of custom and tradition – will reappear again and again, especially in attitudes towards gender and sexual orientation.

Nonetheless, there is some psychological insight in NML, which is that being a good person is related to being a psychologically healthy person – and that psychological health is related to having a positive role within a healthy society. **Utilitarianism** (p10) and **Situation Ethics** (p31) both focus on the individual making decisions in isolation, but Aristotle views moral agents as part of a community and concludes that you cannot discover what makes a good person without also reflecting on what makes a good society.

Telos (Purpose)

In order to work out how to raise children with *aretē* so that they can lead *eudaimon* lives, *Aristotle* argues that we must look for the PURPOSE (or '*telos*') of human life. It's easy enough to see this *telos* in the case of other animals: natural life for birds involves flying, singing, laying eggs, migrating; fish will swim; dogs will bark; etc.

Aristotle argues there is a *telos* for humans too, which involves using our power of RATIONAL THOUGHT, the thing that sets us apart from other animals. The natural life is a rational life.

- It is rational to **keep ourselves alive**
- It is rational to **reproduce**, so that the human race will continue and so that our descendants can carry on our work
- It is rational to **live in an ordered society**, so we can enjoy peace and progress.

> *It might surprise you to think of having sex and making babies as 'rational' but Aristotle doesn't mean 'logical' or 'scientific': he means that this behaviour that **makes sense of our existence** and **gives our lives purpose**.*

Giving in to non-rational desires enslaves and degrades the individual, threatening our security and the security of our society. For example, NML claims it is irrational to steal and tell lies (though it might be profitable and seem rather sensible at times) and it is irrational to live your life entirely for your own happiness. Why?

1. These actions **disrupt society**. A criminal might benefit in the short term, but in the long term even criminals need society to exist in order to enjoy their loot, so **it's irrational to damage the very thing that makes your long-term happiness possible**.
2. We **cannot control the consequences** of our behaviour, so stealing, lying and selfishness are all based on an **illusion** that we can 'fix' things to work out the way we want them to. It is **irrational to chase after illusions** rather than face up to reality.

Thomas Aquinas (p76) explains it like this: people choose APPARENT GOODS that make them happy in the short term (like drunkenness or casual sex) rather than ACTUAL GOODS that secure them long term happiness (like sobriety or chastity). We can tell the difference between these apparent and actual goods by using "**right reason**".

However, the idea of a *telos* for humans has some problems. It's not clear there is such a thing as a single human nature shared by all people. Some feminists argue women have a different nature from men; identity politics argues that different ethnic groups have different natures. It is the *telos* of heterosexuals to marry and reproduce – but do homosexuals have a different *telos* which means they become *eudaimon* by doing different things? Is your nature fixed forever, or can you change your nature, for example as a transsexual seeking gender reassignment?

Biblical foundations

NML begins with Aristotle's ideas in Ancient Greece but its most famous supporter is **Thomas Aquinas (1225-1274)** who bases NML on the Bible.

Aquinas brings in a religious perspective that is missing in Aristotle's work, because Aquinas believes humans are created by God and given a purpose by their Creator. This means there is an ETERNAL LAW, which is God's purpose for the entire universe and everyone in it. Unfortunately, we don't know this Eternal Law and wouldn't understand it even if we discovered it.

Since God is a loving Creator, he reveals portions of his Eternal Law to humans in a direct way. This is DIVINE LAW, which is revealed to prophets (like Moses) and through the life of Jesus Christ. Moslems similarly believe that God's Divine Law is revealed through the Qur'an.

> *If you study **Unit 1 (Philosophy of Religion)**, you might link Natural Law to **general revelation** and Divine Law to **special revelation**; visit:* ***https://philosophydungeon.weebly.com/revelation.html***

Divine Law in the Bible includes things like:

- The **Ten Commandments** (*c.f.* **Exodus 20: 1-17**)
- The **613 *mitzvot*** (commandments) that observant Jews obey, such as avoiding pork and being circumcised
- The **Sermon on the Mount (Matthew 5-7)** and the **Plain (Luke 6)** where Jesus outlines Christian ethics, including **loving your enemies** and the '**Golden Rule**' (*treat others as you wish to be treated*)
- The **Apostolic Decree (Acts 15: 19-21)** is the first moral code of the Early Church, which abandoned the requirement to be circumcised but which instructed Christian converts to avoid sexual immorality, pagan worship and blood offerings

Divine Law is a revealed moral code: there's nothing obvious about it. Humans would not 'work out for themselves' that they should rest on the Sabbath, avoid eating pork or love their enemies.

However, since the world is created by God, it also reflects God's Eternal and so, by studying nature, humans can figure out some of God's purposes: this is NATURAL LAW, which is the portion of Eternal Law that is revealed in nature.

In the Bible, St Paul claims that even Gentiles (non-Jews) who are ignorant of the Divine Law, still know about the Natural Law, since it is part of human nature:

> *They show that the requirements of the law are written on their hearts, their consciences also bearing witness, and their thoughts sometimes accusing them and at other times even defending them* – **Romans 2: 14**

The idea of Natural Law being *"written in men's hearts"* reflect the view that it is human nature to admire some things (like kindness and honesty) but be appalled by other things (like cruelty and treachery).

Thomas Aquinas (pX) argues the NML brings together Natural Law (obvious to all thinking persons) and Divine Law (revealed by God to religious believers):

Absolutism

An important feature of humans having a *telos* (purpose) that makes them *eudaimon* (happy/fulfilled) is that this is an OBJECTIVELY TRUE understanding of human nature. According to NML, it is simply a ***fact*** that some things are natural and good for humans to do – studying, working, getting married, raising children – and other things (like cheating and stealing and cruelty) are unnatural and bad. These bad things are not just relatively bad: they are **absolutely bad** because they go against the very essence of what it is to be human.

The idea that some things are absolutely good or bad, no questions asked, no exceptions, is ABSOLUTISM (p7) and NML is an absolutist ethical theory.

Examples of absolutism include the **Catholic Church**'s rejection of abortion and contraception in all circumstances as well as religions like the **Jehovah's Witnesses** who refuse blood transfusions even in medical emergencies (based on their understanding of the **Apostolic Decree**, p59).

Absolutism is completely lacking in the sort of flexibility that makes **Utilitarianism** (p10) and **Situation Ethics** (p31) so appealing. Many NML theorists would insist that adultery is ***always wrong***, in ***every situation***, for everyone, everywhere, because it is natural (and therefore good) for married partners to be loyal to one another.

- **The Trolley Problem** (p8) is not really a problem for NML. It is absolutely wrong to murder someone, so there is no possible justification for pulling the lever (or pushing the fat man) and the workers on the tracks must be allowed to die.
- **Joseph Fletcher's case study of Mrs Bergmeier** (p42) would not impress a NML theorist. Adultery is immoral so Mrs Bergmeier was wrong to have sex with another man.

On the other hand, absolutism tells people where they stand. It is quite clear what the right and wrong courses of action are – unlike **Utilitarianism** where the wrong course of action might not be obvious until the consequences occur, or **Situation Ethics** where the wrong course of action could be mistaken for the right one if people get confused about the most loving thing to do.

Legalism

Legalism means 'based on laws' and legalistic ethics are moral codes which try to cover every conceivable situation. Deciding on the right thing to do involves working out which law applies to the situation you find yourself in (*c.f.* p7).

Legalism is helpful in ethics but it gives people clear instructions about what to do, instructions which sometimes go against our wishes. It can be contrasted with the vagueness of **Situation Ethics** (p31) or the tendency of **Utilitarianism** (p10) to endorse whatever we feel like doing.

Legalism is useful because it helps formulate real laws – the 'law of the land' or POSITIVE LAW – which are based on moral laws. For example, in the UK, laws used to restrict the opening of shops and the sale of alcohol on Sundays, based on the Commandment to *"remember the Sabbath day by keeping it holy"* (**Exodus 20: 8**).

There are problems with legalism. Treating moral problems as legal problems places intelligence over conscience: people can ignore their consciences because they figure the law is on their side. This can lead to SELF-RIGHTEOUSNESSNESS when people cannot admit they might be wrong.

It can lead to a confusion between moral law and POSITIVE LAW, so that people confuse the 'law of the land' or local customs with morality. But of course, some times the local laws have to be challenged and reformed and local customs (such as how you dress) are not the same thing as timeless moral principles.

There is also the danger of following the LETTER OF THE LAW but ignoring the spirit of the law. This involves applying moral rules in a thoughtless and clumsy way, failing to recognise that the situation demands a more flexible response.

- Jesus' treatment of **the Woman Caught in Adultery (John 8: 3-11**, p36) is often used as a criticism of legalism in ethics

The opposite of legalism is ANTINOMIANISM, the complete rejection of moral laws (p7). **Situation Ethics** tries to find a way between the extremes of legalism and antinomianism.

Legalism is a word with connotations of stupidity and insensitivity. However, maybe any moral code worthy of the name ought to produce **some** *situations where the right thing to do is something you really* **don't want to do**.

PRECEPTS OF NATURAL MORAL LAW

Precepts are general rules for behaviour. **Thomas Aquinas** (*right* and p76) identifies the **Primary Precepts** of NML, which are very general rules. He then works out the **Secondary Precepts** which are more specific and less obvious, but which come from trying to apply the Primary Precepts to human behaviour.

Aquinas agrees with the Ancient Greek philosophers like Aristotle that we live in a purposive world: a world where rational creatures like us have an end, purpose or *telos*. God designed us to use our powers of reason to pursue the *telos* he intends for us, which is to join him in Heaven.

Ultimate goodness is the Eternal Law of God, but a portion of this Eternal Law is present in the mind of each person: this is called SYNDERESIS, which means our innate urge *"to do good and avoid evil."* However, since humans have freewill they can choose to ignore this inner prompting, or become confused about what it is encouraging them to do. This is why they need to use the power of reason to work out moral rules, which is called *"practical wisdom"* or PHRONESIS.

Primary Precepts

Aquinas starts off with the "ideal" human nature. As a Christian, he believes humans have all fallen away from this ideal (as hinted at in the Biblical story of Adam and Eve and the life of Jesus) but he argues that, since it is the ideal, it is the template for the good life.

He produces the **Primary Precepts** of the good life (a mnemonic you can use is PREGS – *see box*). You will notice they are very vague: more like principles than laws or rules.

From these, Aquinas works out **Secondary Precepts**, like not stealing, lying, committing adultery or killing the innocent.

> **PREGS**
> - **P**rotect and preserve human life
> - **R**eproduce and **E**ducate your offspring
> - know **G**od and live in **S**ociety

1. **PROTECT & PRESERVE HUMAN LIFE:** All living things have an instinct to live, so natural law tells us that we should try to protect ourselves and stay alive. We also feel protective of other people and this is natural too. If we were in any doubt about this, divine law reinforces natural law, because **the Ten Commandments** forbid murder (**Exodus 20: 13**).

2. **REPRODUCE:** Animals have a sex drive to reproduce and human beings feel this desire to bring children into a loving relationship. Natural law is strengthened by divine law, because God instructs humans to *"be fruitful and increase in number, multiply upon the earth"* (**Genesis 9: 7**).

3. **EDUCATE YOUR OFFSPRING:** There is a natural urge to protect and nurture children, which is seen in animals (who protect their young until they are old enough to be independent). In humans, this period of nurturing lasts a long time and, since humans are rational animals, they must be educated as well.

4. **KNOW GOD:** This is where Aquinas differs from Aristotle, because he assumes that a religious education (specifically a Christian one) is a Primary Precept too. The point (*telos*) of human life is to serve God on earth and in Heaven – and this *telos* is frustrated if humans are ignorant of Christianity or go to Hell after death.

5. **LIVE IN SOCIETY:** Animals form packs and herds and humans have an inclination to make friendships and neighbourhoods. Natural law is supported by divine law, since God observes that: "*It is not good for man to be alone*" (**Genesis 2: 18**). If it is natural for us to live together in society, it must be wrong to do things that threaten society (like breaking laws and being antisocial).

People seem to love creating mnemonics for the Primary Precepts. If you don't like PREGS, you might prefer POWER: Preserve Life, Ordered Society, Worship God, Education and Reproduction.

It's important to notice how the Precepts all 'hang together' and depend on each other. Preserving your life requires living in an ordered society (which can offer things you can't provide for yourself, like medical help) and reproducing (since your children can care for you when you're old); reproducing also requires an ordered society (for medical help and childcare) and so does education (since you won't possess all the knowledge yourself that you want your children to learn). An ordered society requires its members to preserve their lives and reproduce and value education as a way of passing on its laws and culture to the next generation.

What about **Worshiping God**? Many people will agree with Aquinas about preserving life, raising children and living in an ordered society, but won't see why that has to be a ***religious*** society. Aquinas also presents readers with famous arguments for the existence of God, which he thinks are also based on drawing rational conclusions from the natural world: the **Design Argument** and the **Cosmological Argument** in particular. For Aquinas, we discover moral law in the same way that we discover God's existence and you cannot have one without the other.

*You will study these arguments as part of Unit 1 Philosophy of Religion and you can study them on the Philosophy Dungeon website at **https://philosophydungeon.weebly.com/philosophical-issues--questions.html***

If you reject Aquinas' proofs of God's existence, you could still agree with NML, just remove the **Worship God** Precept. However, since the Precepts 'hang together', NML is weakened. NML assumes that humans have been created with a purpose and that our reasoning mind is a gift from our Creator to figure out that purpose. No Creator means no ultimate purpose. If our power of reasoning is just an evolved trait that happened to have survival value for our ancestors, why should we trust it to tell us how to live our lives?

Secondary Precepts

The Primary Precepts tell us it is natural and good to live together in an ordered society. However, there are lots of different types of ordered society. Nazi Germany was an ordered society. We expect something a bit more specific from an ethical theory.

NML can be applied to particular situations because the Precepts have logical consequences. For example, if it is wrong to kill innocent human beings, it follows that bombing civilian targets (such as Hiroshima in Japan) is wrong. However, killing in self defense is moral, we could justify bombing on these grounds.

Secondary Precepts are ethical rules derived from Primary Precepts using *"practical wisdom"*. Reason tells us that some actions are unnatural and therefore wrong – and wrong in an **absolutist** sense. For example, Aquinas argues that some actions go against the natural purpose (*telos*) of human life. Aquinas gives examples of actions that are wrong because they contradict the Primary Precepts:

- **THEFT:** Stealing is forbidden by divine law (it goes against the 10 Commandments) but it also contradicts the Primary Precept that we should live together in an ordered society. If people steal from each other, trust breaks down and social living becomes impossible.

- **LYING:** According to divine law, the 10 Commandments forbids *"giving false testimony"* which is a type of lying, but lying also contradicts living in an ordered society for the same reason as stealing: it destroys the trust needed for social living to be possible.

- **FORNICATION:** This means 'casual sex' and Aquinas also considers masturbation to be unnatural. This is because the Primary Precepts tell us to reproduce within an ordered society, which means that the purpose (*telos*) of sex is to have children within a marriage and any other use of sex is wrong.

- **ADULTERY:** Having sex when one of you is married to someone else is condemned by divine law (the 10 Commandments) and goes against several Primary Precepts: the *telos* of sex is to raise children in a marriage but adultery goes against this; it also creates distrust in an ordered society because people become suspicious of their spouses and don't know if their children are their own.

- **KILLING THE INNOCENT:** Divine law condemns murder in the 10 Commandments. Aquinas argues in favour of JUST WAR (*c.f.* **Unit 3, Applications of Ethical Theories**) but, in general, killing people goes against the Precept to preserve life. However, living in an ordered society might only be possible if some people are killed in self-defence. Aquinas concludes there is only an absolute rule against killing ***innocent*** people (and for Aquinas, this includes **aborting unborn babies**).

These Secondary Precepts and others like them are worked out by reflecting on the logical demands of respecting the Primary Precepts and assuming that there is a specific purpose (*telos*) behind every human behaviour. However, they are mot Primary Precepts themselves, so there might be circumstances where the Secondary Precepts don't apply.

APPLICATION OF NATURAL MORAL LAW

When we apply the Secondary Precepts to particular situations, they often conflict with each other. For example, a Secondary Precept tells you to keep your promises but another Precept tells you to help your friends. If a friend asks for your help but you've already promised your help to someone else, which law do you follow?

CASUISTRY is a technique for deciding which ethical laws apply to your situation, usually by working out whether some laws take precedence over others. For example, many ethicists would conclude the duty to keep your promise is greater than the duty to help a friend.

Casuistry has some negative connotations. Critics during the Enlightenment used 'casuistry' to refer to the way some Catholic thinkers seemed to make their religion justify just about anything, including some things that were clearly evil. However, in *The Abuse of Casuistry* **(1988)**, the philosophers **Jonson & Toulmin** argue that casuistry is still an important ethical tool..

DOUBLE EFFECT (DE) is an example of casuistry in action. DE refers to choices that lead to two possible outcomes, one intended and the other foreseeable but not intended. According to NML, you are only morally responsible for the things you **foresee and intend**, not for things you didn't foresee or didn't intend.

DE means there are circumstances where the Secondary Precepts don't apply:

- **The act must be a *good* one:** DE cannot be used to justify something that goes directly against the Primary Precepts, but self-defense is in line with the Primary Precepts and so is carrying out a medical operation
- **The good outcome must not be the result of the bad outcome:** DE cannot be used 'in hindsight' to justify something bad
- **The intention must be good:** This is important: the person must genuinely intend a good outcome.
- **It must be for serious reasons:** Going against the Secondary Precepts is a serious business and it must be over something important.

If a pregnant woman needs life-saving surgery, a surgeon might foresee the possibility that the surgery will cause her to miscarry her unborn child. The act is a good one (surgery) and it comes before any unfortunate consequences (miscarriage), the intention is good (to save the mother's life) and it's a serious reason.

However, abortion cannot be justified using DE. The act is a bad one (killing an innocent human life). The intention is not good (it's specifically to kill the foetus) and even if the abortion benefits the mother in various ways (such as removing stress and worry from her life), that good outcome is a result of the death of the foetus.

DE can be applied to **Joseph Fletcher's case studies** (p38) with very different results from the ones **Situation Ethics** would recommend:

- **Himself Might His Quietus Make (p39):** Euthanasia cannot be justified with DE. The act (killing yourself) is bad and the bad outcome is the cause of the good one (an insurance payout for the family). This is true even if the reasons are serious and the intention is good (to secure your family's happiness after your death).
- **Special Bombing Mission No.13 (p40):** Bombing innocent civilians in war is contrary to the Primary Precepts. The atomic bombing of Japanese cities was not carried out in self-defense and even if it brought the war to a quick end, this is a good outcome resulting directly from the bad outcome (two cities destroyed).
- **Christian Cloak & Dagger (p41):** The Primary Precepts state sex is for reproduction within a loving marriage, so using sex to blackmail someone can never be justified by DE, even if the intention is good and there are serious reasons (like stopping a war).
- **Sacrificial Adultery (p42):** Similarly, DE cannot justify sex being used to get a mother released from prison and reunited with her family, since this goes against the *telos* of sex: Mrs Bergmeier's good intentions don't justify her adultery and the good outcome is once again the result of the bad one.

Contemporary applications

The Catholic Church continues to use NML to support its ethical teachings, including opposition to divorce, contraception, abortion and euthanasia.

NML has influences beyond Catholicism. In his famous *Letter from a Birmingham Jail* **(1963)**, civil rights activist **Martin Luther King Jr** uses NML to defend his campaign of civil disobedience against racism in America.

> *There are two types of laws: just and unjust. I would be the first to advocate obeying just laws. One has not only a legal but a moral responsibility to obey just laws. Conversely, one has a moral responsibility to disobey unjust laws* – **Martin Luther King Jr**

King makes a distinction between the 'law of the land' (POSITIVE LAW) and the deeper moral law (*c.f.* p59), arguing that any law not rooted in "*eternal law and natural law*" is unjust, but any law that "*uplifts human personality*" is a just law. The 'Jim Crow Laws' in the USA forced black Americans to live outside of mainstream society: this crushes the human personality and so these laws were unjust.

> *An individual who breaks a law that conscience tells him is unjust … is in reality expressing the highest respect for law* – **Martin Luther King Jr**

> *You studied Dr King as a Key Scholar for the **Ethics of Equality** in **Topic 1** - covered in **Significant Concepts in Religion & Ethics**. You could make a link between NML and equality in your essays.*

NML is often used to justify non-violent protest because it provides a platform by which the laws of a country can be evaluated 'from the outside'. NML offers a way to criticise countries and communities and challenge them to improve themselves.

NML is often expressed in the language of HUMAN RIGHTS. The Primary Precepts are taken to mean that, being the sort of creatures they are, humans have a right to life, to a family, to an education, to freedom of worship and to movement and expression in society.

Hugo Grotius (1584-1645, *right*) was a Dutch scholar who used NML to formulate the idea of INTERNATIONAL LAW, which provides a standard all countries must abide by. In the 21st century, these ideas are represented by the **International Court** (which can put the rulers of countries on trial), the **Geneva Conventions** (which imposes rules on conduct in war) and the **United Nations**, whose purpose is to *"promote and encourage respect for human rights and for fundamental freedoms for all without distinction as to race, sex, language, or religion."*

Despite this, NML often finds itself in conflict with many 21st century attitudes.

- **Gender roles:** Many NML thinkers conclude that certain gender roles are natural and therefore moral duties. For example, men should be breadwinners and women should be homemakers. This understanding of gender is opposed by **feminists**, who view most gender roles as social constructions (i.e. gender is part of Positive Law, not Natural Law).
- **Homosexuality:** By contrast, NML thinkers often view homosexuality as unnatural and wrong and do not accept that anyone is 'born gay'. This is because NML proposes a single human nature and a single *telos* for sex which a reproduction (only possible for heterosexual sex).
- **Transsexuality:** Similarly, NML views biological sex as assigned at birth and the basis for gender: transsexuality is seen as unnatural and therefore wrong.
- **Conservation:** NML is concerned with the *telos* of humans, who are viewed as **ontologically distinct** (different sorts of beings) from animals. Christian NML thinkers argue that humans are *imago Dei* ('in the image of God') but animals are not. This means that the Primary Precepts do not apply to animals and they have no rights.

Because of this, NML is often viewed as 'out of step' with contemporary thought. Although NML has championed many basic rights and promoted concepts like the SANCTITY OF LIFE, it often opposes the advancement of LGBT rights, animal rights and women's suffrage.

> *In Topic 1 (Significant Concepts in Religion & Ethics), you studied Environment Ethics and the Ethics of Equality - you should review those topics now and reflect on how NML compares to perspectives like Utilitarianism and Kantianism.*

Proportionalism

Since the 1960s there have been many challenges to traditional views of the moral law. There has been greater equality for women, greater tolerance for homosexuality and transsexuality and a growing sense that there is no single 'right way to live'. **Relativism** (p7) is the view that morality is just an individual opinion, not a law that applies to everyone. Many people today view moral problems as things that don't have a single solution that applies to everyone.

Proportionalism is a reaction against the strongly **legalistic** and **absolutist** character of NML. **Richard McCormick (1922–2000)**, a Jesuit priest and moral theologian, condemns *"an excessively casuistic approach to the moral life"* which he feels is typical of Catholic ethics. By 'casuistic' McCormick means the way Catholics treat the Precepts as absolutes and use techniques like DOUBLE EFFECT (p65) to create occasional 'wiggle room' in extreme situations.

He argues instead for a more flexible approach to the Precepts themselves:

> *Every moral choice occurs in a context where competing values and disvalues must be weighed critically* – **Richard McCormick**

Bernard Hoose (p79) is a Key Scholar for this Topic who argues that NML should be viewed as a framework or guideline for making moral decisions, not a set of inflexible rules. He suggests that people should take into account the ***proportion*** of good and bad consequences that will come from following Precepts and abandon the Precept if the evil significantly outweighs the good.

McCormick and Hoose distinguish between different types of evil and good:

- **Pre-moral Evil:** This is something obviously and objectively bad (e.g. stabbing someone with a knife) and it does not take intentions into account.

  Proportionalists reject the idea viewing things as **pre-moral evil** because intentions *always* matter (e.g. a surgeon cuts people with a knife, but does this while trying to help their patient).

- **Ontic Evil:** This is the idea that we live in a imperfect 'Fallen' world (perhaps because of the sin of Adam and Eve in **Genesis 3**) and this explains natural disasters, tragic accidents and the way even good intentions can turn out to be harmful.

  Ontic Evil is the reason why **absolute and legalistic** approaches to ethics do not work out. The universe is **morally ambiguous** and good actions can lead to evil and evil actions can lead to good. Even though the 10 Commandments forbid murder, there will be circumstances where it may be proportionate to break this commandment (e.g. to protect innocent people from a terrorist).

- **Evil Moral Act:** This is an action which is ***actually*** bad

  Bernard Hoose argues that, since we always need to take circumstances and intentions into account, we cannot state in advance whether something is going to be an Evil Moral Act; if a pre-moral action has proportionate moral justification, it might NOT be an Evil Moral Act.

- **Good Act:** Following a moral rule (like the Secondary Precepts) **and** having the right intentions.

  Bernard Hoose agrees with **Joseph Fletcher** (p78) that the best intention that makes an action a Good Act is *agápē* (love).

- **Right Act:** Breaking a moral rule, but for **proportionate reasons**, to bring about the 'lesser of two evils' or the least-bad consequences.

  For example, stealing a gun with the intention of stopping a terrorist from killing innocent people cannot be a Good Act (because Secondary Precept was broken – stealing) but it might be a Right Act (since it is better than letter the terrorist carry out his evil plan).

Because of Ontic Evil, we often have to settle for doing Right Acts rather than doing Good Acts. There is an old expression that goes '***The Best is often the enemy of the Good***'. This means that sometimes our desire to do what's best backfires, because the best course of action might be very difficult or even outright impossible. Often, we are better off doing 'second best' and doing it well. This seems to be Proportionalism's challenge to NML. Instead of trying to live by absolutist laws, we should sometimes **compromise** by doing Right Acts instead of Good Acts.

Proportionalism is a more flexible approach than the Catholic Church's **absolutist** opposition to abortion, contraception, homosexuality and divorce. For example, a couple might wish to use contraception if the woman has a medical condition (like a heart defect) which would put her life in danger were she to become pregnant. Currently, Catholic NML would require the couple to risk the woman's health or abstain from sex completely rather than use unnatural contraception. Proportionalists argue that, though using contraception is not a Good Act, for a couple in this situation it might nonetheless be the Right Act.

Proportionalism could be seen as the Catholic version of **Situation Ethics** (p31) and shares many of the strengths and weaknesses of Situationalism. In particular, Proportionalism takes a pessimistic view of how effective it is trying to follow ethical rules in a legalistic way and has an optimistic view of people's ability to navigate their way through ethical problems once they set the strict rules aside. However, it is also open to **William Barclay**'s criticism that it is an ethical idea only for "*saints*" and that it offers ordinary people "a *terrifying degree of freedom*" (p52).

Moreover, Proportionalism has been condemned by the Catholic Church. **Pope John Paul II (1920-2005**, *right***)** opposed Hoose's ideas in *Veritatis Splendor* **(1993,** *The Splendour of Truth***).**

The Pope points out (correctly) that Proportionalism denies that any action is intrinsically evil. In other words, Proportionalism is a **relativistic** ethical theory and the Pope advises Catholics to reject it in favour of traditional NML.

In 2010, **Pope Benedict** blamed the spread of Proportionalist ideas among Catholics for the sexual abuse scandal that engulfed the Catholic Church. Benedict sums up Proportionalism's 'bad influence' like this:

> *It was maintained – even within the realm of Catholic theology – that there is no such thing as evil in itself or good in itself. There is only a 'better than' and a 'worse than'. Nothing is good or bad in itself* **– Pope Benedict**

It is a bit far-fetched to blame Proportionalism for priests sexually abusing people in their congregations, but it illustrates how opposed to Proportionalism the Popes have been.

However, the current **Pope Francis** is viewed by some commentators as more well-disposed towards Proportionalism. He certainly warns Catholics about the dangers of *"legalism"* and *"inflexibility"* and these are concerns shared by Proportionalists.

Another argument employed by Proportionalists is that moral behaviour is something individuals have to work out for themselves. They accuse traditional NML (especially in its Catholic variety) of trying to provide a rule for every situation in life, so that individuals don't have to think for themselves. Many people behave morally out of fear, or a lack of imagination, or simply to fit in and be popular. Bernard Hoose questions whether there is anything particularly ethical about living like this.

Charlotte Vardy illustrates this criticism with the example of a mother teaching her teenage child to drive. One sort of mother tries to *"eliminate all risk"* by dictating everything you do; the other sort *"sits next to you and lets you practise on her car"* because she wants you to learn to drive solo. Traditional (Catholic) NML is like the over-controlling mother, but Proportionalism claims people really need the more trusting sort.

EVALUATING NATURAL MORAL LAW

Natural Moral Law is a powerful contribution to ethical thought. It is an **absolutist** (p7, 60) and **deontological** (p6) ethical theory. This means it offers people a strict and rather pure standard to live their lives by and it doesn't compromise this standard to fit with particular situations. May feel that this is what ethics should be like: holding yourself to an ideal and living by a strict code.

The strict principles of NML give people very clear guidance as moral agents: it's very obvious what behaviour follows these principles and what behaviour breaks them. This means people know when they are doing wrong. Everything is clear cut. In contrast, there is a wooliness to **Situation Ethics** (p31) and with **Utilitarianism** (p10) it might not be clear whether you did the right thing until the consequences happen.

NML is based on reasoning from observations about human experience. This makes it an **objective** theory – if everyone reasons correctly we all come to the same conclusions about what is right and wrong. There is evidence for this: all across the world, in every society, people condemn murder and theft, rape and incest, promise-breaking and cruelty.

However, there are cultural differences in ethics too. Some cultures allow a man to have many wives, some are tolerant of homosexuality while others condemn it, some celebrate war, others see no problem with torture. NML theorists would say this is because **Positive Law** (local ethical codes) is not the same as the true Moral Law. There is a need for **moral progress**. NML can criticise social customs, local laws and prejudices and bringing about reform. NML views the actual law we have and the moral code people live by as a 'work in progress' – it always needs improving. In contrast, **Situation Ethics** and **Utilitarianism** both encourage **relativism**, which is the idea that right and wrong are relative terms and we are in no position to criticise a society or a community for the way that it behaves.

Aquinas and other NML philosophers do not claim to know, absolutely, what the Moral Law is; there will always be disagreements about what behaviour is *actually* good. They just insist that, beyond these disagreements, there is *in fact* an absolute Moral Law. Nazi war criminals were condemned for their 'crimes against humanity', a phrase that is based on the idea of Natural Law and is a good example of deontological ethics standing outside national interests and providing a standard by which whole countries can be judged.

The idea of 'human nature' is controversial for NML. This applies to all humans, regardless of sex, race or ability. The Catholic Church uses this argument to defend the life of foetuses and argue against euthanasia on the grounds that the sick, handicapped or unwanted share our common human nature and must be protected. The idea of an unchanging human nature underlies HUMAN RIGHTS – a way of life for humans in which they can flourish and which requires safety, education and freedom of expression. Societies that enslave their women or treat racial minorities as second-class citizens are preventing people from living in a fully human way.

Some critics of NML are sceptical about 'human nature' itself. Is there really one way of life that is 'natural' for all humans? Obviously, most of us think the way of life we've grown up in is 'natural' but people who grow up with cannibalism and human sacrifice presumably find that 'natural' too. There is a range of competing ideas about what is 'natural'. Strict followers of the **Bible** and the **Qur'an** would say it's 'natural' for women to stay home, keep house and have babies; Feminists would say it's 'natural' for women to do anything men do and old-fashioned gender roles are just human inventions (i.e. Positive Law), not 'natural' at all.

Another criticism is leveled at the idea of looking for a *telos* (purpose) in all aspects of human experience. For example, human teeth include canines (for tearing meat) and molars (for grinding vegetables). Does this make it unnatural to eat a meal with no meat in it? Or a meal that consists only of meat? Another example is human sexuality. Thomas Aquinas himself admits that some people should give up sex to become monks and nuns, but isn't this unnatural? What about women with intelligence to pursue careers: isn't it unnatural for them not to use their talents if they stay home and raise babies? The *telos* of a mouth is to eat food: does this make kissing unnatural?

The whole idea of 'purpose' in nature is connected to the **Design Argument for the existence of God** (*c.f.* **Unit 1 Philosophy of Religion**), which was also promoted by Thomas Aquinas. However, since the 18th century, philosophers have criticised this idea. Modern science does not look for 'purpose' in nature.

Richard Dawkins (*right*) titled his book on evolution ***The Blind Watchmaker*** **(1986)**, representing the idea that nature seems to be like a watchmaker (creating complicated systems and organisms) but is really 'blind' (operating with no plan or purpose).

In contrast, NML is strongly linked to religion. Some thinkers try to ditch the religious aspect of NML; modern human rights would be an example of NML without God. However, without the idea of an Eternal Law, the distinction between Natural Law and Positive Law breaks down. 'Natural' becomes 'whatever your society says is good'. For example, the Nazis thought it was natural – and therefore good – to wipe out 'lesser races' like Jews, Gypsies and Slavs as well as homosexuals and the mentally handicapped.

In the world today, Europe and the USA try to impose their ideas about the human rights of women and minorities on other countries; many of these countries regard 'human rights' as an excuse used by the rich powerful countries to boss them about. China, in particular, would argue that it is doing fine without human rights. This illustrates the key problem with NML: who is to say what the *telos* is of human life is? If reason cannot solve this question, then religious believers resort to saying that this purpose is revealed in the Bible.

Compatibility with religious approaches

NML combines the moral codes in the Bible with moral principles humans can work out for themselves. It is associated with Catholic ethics but many other Christian groups follow NML in less strict ways. For example, The **Richard Hooker (1554-1600)** adapted NML for the **Church of England**: to live, to learn, to reproduce, to worship God, and to live in an ordered society

Other theistic religions (religions that believe in a Creator God) follow their own equivalents of NML. **Islam** also offers a code of laws revealed by God (in the **Qur'an**) combined with moral teachings that humans can work out for themselves (codified by Muslim judges as part of **Sharia Law**). This has many similarities with Catholic NML, such as rules for marriage, forbidding homosexuality and commending honesty, generosity and family values.

Eastern religions do not tend to believe in a Creator God who reveals his moral laws to humans. However, they still believe in the equivalent of Eternal Law: a way of living that goes beyond human existence and is in harmony with the universe. This is often referred to as **the Tao** (meaning 'the Way' and rhyming with 'cow').

> [The Tao] *is Nature, it is the Way, the Road. It is the Way in which the universe goes on, the Way in which things everlastingly emerge, stilly and tranquilly, into space and time. It is also the Way which every man should tread in imitation* – **C.S. Lewis (1944)**

In **Hinduism** and **Buddhism**, the pattern that ethical living must follow is called **the Dharma**. The Dharma is illustrated in Hindu sacred texts like the **Upanishads** and the **Vedas**, but it can be worked out from reflecting on nature, life and death – and especially through meditation. It consists of self-control, non-aggression and honesty. In Buddhism, the Dharma is illustrated in the **Eightfold Noble Path** of ethical living and especially in the instruction to be non-violent (*ahimsa*). Buddhists refer to goodness as 'skillful' behaviour (*kusala*) because this is behaviour which 'fits' with the supreme pattern of reality. Evil is 'unskillful' (*akusala*): it is living life in a clumsy, ignorant way that produces suffering in yourself and the people around you.

In Western theistic religions, God is both the law-giver and the judge who will punish people who break the moral law. In Eastern religions, the law is self-policing through **karma** which means that those who break the law attract suffering to themselves, in this life or in a future reincarnation.

However, religions have other ethical teachings which conflict with NML. For example, in Christianity, there is the 'Law of Love' (*agápē*) which instructs people to show compassionate love for each other. **Situation Ethics** (p31) and **Proportionalism** (p68) both emphasise the importance of expressing love as an alternative to following moral rules.

Other religions focus on DIVINE COMMANDS rather than Natural Law: these are instructions which are to be followed simply because they are believed to be from God, not because they are natural or beneficial for humans. Some Christian groups follow Divine Commands (as they see them) to refuse blood transfusions (**Jehovah's Witnesses**) or drink coffee (**Mormons**). **Muslims** and **Jews** refuse to eat pork; **Muslims** do not drink alcohol. Sometimes Divine Commands are viewed as tests of commitment or proofs of devotion to God, rather than acts which promote human flourishing, which is the basic idea of NML.

Changes to Law & Social Attitudes

The Catholic Church's commitment to NML led it to oppose – but not to end – slavery. There is no condemnation of slavery in the Bible, but since ancient times Christians have felt slavery to be incompatible with the idea of the equality of all believers. **Thomas Aquinas** approved of slavery as a punishment for certain crimes, but not slavery that could be inherited from your parents. After the discovery of the Americas, the Catholic Church condemned the enslavement of native peoples in 1537. In 1741, the Catholic Church condemned the Atlantic trade in African slaves too.

Other non-Catholic groups protested against slavery, arguing that, above and beyond 'the law of the land' (Positive Law) there is a 'higher law' (Natural Law) by which human laws can be judged. This appeal to a 'higher law' links the abolitionists who opposed slavery, the Civil Rights activists of the 20th century, Climate Change activists today and even the conspirators who plotted to assassinate Adolf Hitler during WWII.

However, the Church failed to take a hard line on slavery (because it involved confronting wealthy patrons and the rulers of countries); it was the Protestant groups like the **Methodists** and **Quakers** who campaigned successfully against slavery in the UK and USA in the 19th century. Only in 1995 did **Pope John Paul II** finally condemn all forms of slavery.

Catholic NML's failure to act against slavery might be because slavery doesn't clearly violate the Primary Precepts. Freedom is not a Primary Precept and slaves can still live, reproduce, be educated, worship and live in an orderly society; indeed, supporters of slavery used to argue that an orderly society depended on slaves. This shows how, while NML can support moral progress *in theory*, it often ends up backing the *status quo* and resisting anything that might destabilize an 'orderly society'.

> The link between NML and the ending of slavery is useful for you when responding to **Religion Equality** in **Topic 1 Selected Concepts in Ethics**.

Other causes draw inspiration from the idea of Natural Law: the extremists who support imposing Islamic codes through violence are also appealing to a 'higher law' and so do the white supremacists who attacking immigrants and ethnic minorities. This shows that an 'orderly society' is not necessarily a desirable thing if it requires ethnic cleansing or religious warfare.

NML often opposes other moral reforms. For example, the Catholic Church opposes women priests and gay relationships. Partly, this is because the Catholic Church appeals to Divine Law as well as Natural Law, and the Bible has some fairly clear things to say about the supporting role of women and the wrongness of homosexuality.

This is an old problem with **Deontology** (p6): following rules for rules' sake can lead to evil outcomes. For example, the Catholic Church opposes contraception because it is unnatural, but this leads to banning condoms in countries suffering from over-population or AIDS.

This problem becomes clear in the debate about homosexuality. The NML view is that there is something unnatural about homosexuality, since people 'should' be heterosexual in order to fulfil their purpose as humans (eg to reproduce). However, homosexuals argue they are 'born this way', that homosexuality is part of their nature and it would be unnatural for them to deny it and try to repress it. Science is used by both sides to defend their position.

NML has certainly declined in influence. In the 21st century, many people support IDENTITY POLITICS, which is the idea that different groups (ethnic minorities, sexual orientations, genders) have their own essential nature and there isn't a single human nature that everyone participates in and must conform to. The good life for a straight white man might not be the good life for a black gay woman. This shift in thinking about human nature is good for diversity but makes it hard to support **objectivity** in ethics or the idea of a 'higher law' that applies to all people everywhere.

Nevertheless, some thinkers argue for a return to NML. The French philosopher **Jacques Maritain (1882-1973**, *right***)** argues that NML is the only ethical theory that can criticise and resist TOTALITARIAN regimes like Communism and Fascism which try to define good and evil as whatever that state wants them to be; relativistic theories like **Utilitarianism** (p10) end up going along with totalitarian states because they offer people security at the expense of their freedoms.

Maritain's ideas about *"the dignity of the human person"* contributed to the **United Nations Declaration of Human Rights (1948)**. However, Maritain views NML as an evolving idea, not a fixed set of rights:

> *No declaration of human rights will ever be exhaustive and final* – **Jacques Maritain (1947)**

These issues are growing in importance. In 2019, massive protests were triggered in **Hong Kong** when the Chinese government introduced new laws to extradite Hong Kong citizens to China to stand trial. These protests oppose the idea that the Chinese government can pass any laws it likes: there is a 'higher law' that even the powerful Chinese Communist Party cannot go against, and this includes freedom. Some of the protestors chanted slogans such as: *"The police are breaking the law"* (**source: New York Times, July 2019**); this insight comes from NML and links back to **Martin Luther King Jr**'s famous *Letter from a Birmingham Jail* (**1963**, p66).

KEY SCHOLARS

Thomas Aquinas

Topic: 2.3 Natural Moral Law

Thomas Aquinas (1225-1274) was the great Christian thinker who merged Aristotelian ideas with Christianity. His greatest work was the *Summa Theologica* (**1274**, unfinished at his death**)**. The *Summa* is a massive book, at three and a half thousand pages, and includes Aquinas' thoughts on proving the existence of God (*c.f.* **Unit 1 - Philosophy of Religion**), but the material on ethics is from Books I-II. He is also the Key Scholar for **Topic 3.1 (War & Peace)**.

In THOMIST philosophy ('*Thomist*' means related to Thomas Aquinas), God is the final end (*telos*) for all human beings and all human beings share the same nature, since we were all created IMAGO DEI (*"in the image of God"*). Aquinas considers alternative goals for human life (pleasure, knowledge) but finds them inadequate (pleasure only satisfies the body while knowledge can only be reached by the educated few).

The problem is that people choose "apparent goods" that make them happy in the short term (like drunkenness or fornication) rather than "actual goods" that secure them long term happiness (like sobriety or chastity). We can tell the difference between these apparent and actual goods by using "**right reason**".

> *Good is to be done and promoted and evil to be avoided* – **Thomas Aquinas**

For Aquinas, we do not invent morals, we *discover* them. The ultimate morality is **Eternal Law**, which is the goodness of God. This is beyond human understanding, but God makes portions of the Eternal Law obvious to us through **revelation**, such as the Ten Commandments: this is the **Divine Law** (p59). God's Eternal Law makes itself known in other ways, because God is the Creator of the universe. This is the **Natural Law** we can discover through reason, by thinking about what makes for a happy, flourishing human life (p58). So, for example, you don't need to be a Christian or read the Bible to work out that a life of drunkenness and casual sex will not, in the long run, make anyone happy or fulfilled.

Humans then set up their own laws and social conventions, based on Natural Law, maybe mixed with bits of Divine Law: this is **Positive Law** which is a human creation and therefore imperfect. For example, in the past Positive Law discriminated against women but over the centuries clearer thinking about Natural Law and Divine Law has led to greater equality for women.

Another important contribution made by Aquinas is the difference between INTERIOR acts and EXTERIOR acts – intentions matter more than consequences. Giving money to the poor so that people can praise and admire you is doing the right thing for the wrong reason. Good intentions are much more important, even if the exterior act (giving money to a beggar) works out badly (say, because he spends it on alcohol).

Jeremy Bentham

Topic: 2.1 Utilitarianism

Jeremy Bentham (1748-1832) is known as the 'father of Utilitarianism'. Bentham was a lawyer and social reformer who campaigned to improve prison conditions and also for better treatment of animals and equaity between the sexes.

Bentham introduced Utilitarianism in his *Introduction to the Principles of Morals and Legislation* (1789), in which he worked out the PRINCIPLE OF UTILITY: actions are good if they promote the greatest amount of happiness. He identifies happiness with pleasure and the absence of pain.

> *It is the greatest happiness of the greatest number that is the measure of right and wrong*
> **– Jeremy Bentham**

This is also known as the '**greatest happiness principle**'. Bentham believed that human beings (and other animals) are fundamentally motivated by pleasure: even actions which don't seem to be motivated by pleasure boil down to pleasure-seeking in the end. For example, even someone who devotes their time to charity and gives away their money does so because they *enjoy* behaving this way and they 'get a kick out of it'. Bentham argues that pleasure and pain "*govern us in all we do, in all we say, in all we think.*" This view is PSYCHOLOGICAL EGOISM and it is a Bentham learned it from the earlier philosopher, **Thomas Hobbes (1588-1679)**.

Psychological egoism is not a widely accepted theory and it's not necessary to agree with Bentham on this to support Utilitarianism. In fact, later utilitarians like **J.S. Mill** (p15, 80) and **Peter Singer** (p22) move away from psychological egoism and the focus on pleasure to interpret Utilitarianism more about happiness, flourishing and justice.

Bentham adopted the term 'utility' from the Scottish philosopher **David Hume (1711-1776)**. Hume argues that having a certain sort of moral character (a 'good personality') has utility because it makes social life more pleasant. Bentham applies this to thinking about particular actions having pleasant or unpleasant consequences.

Bentham was a fierce opponent of religion and religious ethics. He rejected the deontological idea that actions could be **intrinsically** wrong (or wrong-in-themselves). For Bentham, actions could only be **instrumentally** wrong: wrong because they led to unhappy consequences. Bentham was a supporter of LEGAL REFORM and argued that, because circumstances are always changing and the law has to change to keep up with them.

In Bentham's lifetime, the **French Revolution (1787-1799)** shocked Europe, at first because the French people executed their aristocrat rulers in the name of HUMAN RIGHTS and later because of 'the Terror' that followed when ordinary people were imprisoned, tortured and executed. Bentham promoted Utilitarianism to oppose (what seemed to him to be) the dangerous idea of human rights, which he considered to be "*nonsense on stilts*"!

Bentham assembled a group of 'Philosophic Radicals' to promote social reform in Britain without the chaos and suffering brought about by the Revolution in France. One of these radicals was James Mill, the father of **J.S. Mill** (p15, 80).

Joseph Fletcher

Topic: 2.2 Situation Ethics

Situation Ethics (p31) was pioneered by **Joseph Fletcher (1905-1991)** in his book **Situation Ethics: The New Morality (1966)**. Fletcher was ordained an Episcopal priest, but also a supporter of euthanasia and abortion. He claims he was inspired by a St Louis cab driver who said to a passenger: *"Sometimes you've gotta push your principles to one side and do the right thing"*. Fletcher realised that having principles (fixed rules) isn't the same thing as doing what is right.

> *Since 'circumstances alter cases', Situationalism holds that in practice what in some times and places we call right is in other times and places wrong* – **Joseph Fletcher**

Fletcher argues for the importance of the Christian idea of **agápē** in ethcs (p33).

> *We ought to love people and use things; the essence of immorality is to love things and use people* – **Joseph Fletcher**

Fletcher proposes 6 **Fundamental Principles** for **Situation Ethics** (p31):

1. **Love only is always good.** Love is **intrinsically** valuable; it is worthwhile for its own sake. A lie is not intrinsically wrong. For the Situationalist, what makes the lie right is its loving purpose (eg to protect someone's feelings). This approach to ethics puts MOTIVES at the centre of ethical decision-making, unlike **Utilitarianism** (p10), which looks only at consequences.
2. **Love is the only norm (rule).** Love replaces the idea of a moral law. The moral law should only be obeyed in the interests of love, not for its own sake. Fletcher rejects **Natural Law** (p57). He says *'There are no [natural] universal laws held by all men everywhere at all times.'* This is why we have a follow **relative**, not **absolute**, moral rules.
3. **Love and justice are the same.** Fletcher argues that love *requires* justice. If you take examples of injustice – a child starving, an innocent man arrested and condemned, etc – Fletcher argues these show lack of love: if love was shared, there would be no injustice.
4. **Love is not liking.** Love is discerning and critical, not sentimental. **Martin Luther King** described *agápē* as a *'creative, redemptive goodwill to all men'*. He said it would be nonsense to ask people to **like** their violent oppressors. Fletcher agrees with this: *"Love wills the neighbour's good whether we like him or not."* In other words, Situation Ethics isn't about your **feelings**; it's about treating everyone **as if** you loved them.
5. **Love justifies the means.** Deontologists like to say *'The end doesn't justify the means'*, but Fletcher's reply is *'Then what on earth does?'*. Fletcher says you can't claim to be motivated by love if you are causing suffering to people.
6. **Love decides there and then.** Most of the time, *agápē* will tell you to follow normal moral rules, but sometimes it will tell you to break those rules. Utilitarianism has a similar idea that it's important to be flexible, but Fletcher says that *agápē* gives us a clearer sense of when we need to follow a rule and when we need to break it than **hedonic calculus** can (p11)

In his later life, Fletcher declared himself to be an **atheist**. This does not undermine his ideas about ethics, but it perhaps supports criticisms that Situation Ethics is not in line with Christian beliefs about God.

Bernard Hoose

Topic: 2.3 Natural Moral Law

Bernard Hoose is a Catholic ethicist who challenged traditional Catholic ethics with his 1987 book: ***Proportionalism: The American Debate and its European Roots***. He calls this ethical idea **Proportionalism** (p68), which has many similarities with **Situation Ethics** (p31) because Hoose writes: "*an action born of love cannot be wrong.*"

Hoose argues that, in a world where all humans are sinners and **Ontic Evil** (p68) causes even the best intentions to work out badly, any moral decision-making has to be about COMPROMISE, rather than sticking to some perfect standard. Proportionalism says we should aim for the greater good (or the lesser evil), rather than Goodness itself:

> *We need to take into account all the goods and evils that are involved … taking into account unintended but foreseeable side-effects of our actions* – **Bernard Hoose**

Hoose isn't suggesting we make up moral rules as we go along: he's still within the **NML** tradition (p57). What he says is that we should be prepared to break the **Secondary Precepts** of NML (p64) in those cases where they contradict the **Primary Precepts** (p62).

> *It is never right to go against a principle unless there is a proportionate reason which would justify it* – **Bernard Hoose**

Hoose claims that he is not challenging the ideas of **Thomas Aquinas** (p76); rather, he claims to be more faithful to them than the modern Catholic Church is. Aquinas famously argued that sometimes it was morally acceptable for a starving man to steal bread if he was dying of hunger, because the Primary Precept (*preserving human life*) is more important than the Secondary Precept (*do not steal*). Hoose argues this shows that Aquinas didn't employ the technique of **Double Effect** (DE, p65) very strictly, because when you steal food to survive the stealing (which breaks the Secondary Precept) is the cause of you having enough food to live.

Hoose concludes that we can be much more flexible about how we follow the Primary Precepts than the Catholic Church currently allows, but he is still an **absolutist** (p7, 60) about the Primary Principles themselves.

> *We should always do only what, in conscience, we judge to be morally right, and we should never do what we judge in conscience to be morally wrong* – **Bernard Hoose**

Supporters of Hoose claim that Aquinas never intended NML to be interpreted in a **legalistic** and **absolutist** way (pp60-61). However, in Catholicism, the Secondary Precepts are treated as absolutes and cannot be questioned.

Proportionalism was condemned by the Catholic Church. **Pope John Paul II (1920-2005)** states that Proportionalism is wrong because there are some acts which are always wrong in and of themselves – they are **intrinsically evil**. In reply, Hoose says:

> *What the Proportionalists have done is point out the inconsistency and invalidity of such thinking* – **Bernard Hoose**

John Stuart Mill

Topic: 2.1 Utilitarianism

John Stuart Mill (1806-1873) was the son of the philosopher James Mill, who one of Bentham's 'Philosophic Radicals' (p77) and the God-son of Bentham himself. He carried on Bentham's concerns with social reform and Utilitarianism. Mill restates Bentham's PRINCIPLE OF UTILITY:

> *Actions are right in proportion as they tend to promote happiness; wrong as they tend to produce the reverse of happiness* – **J.S. Mill**

Just as Bentham developed Utilitarianism in opposition to the rights-based ethic promoted by the French revolutionaries, Mill argued for Utilitarianism in opposition to another European theory: INTUITIONISM. This theory, popular in Germany and derived from the ideas of **Immanuel Kant** (*c.f.* **Topic 5**), argued that good and evil were objective truths that could be sensed using the power of **intuition** (or moral feelings). Mill viewed this as a way of defending the *status quo* against reformers (like himself) who wanted to change things.

Mill sets out his ideas in his book, ***Utilitarianism* (1863)**, which has been identified as:

> *the most famous defense of the utilitarian view ever written* – **Geoffrey Scarre (2002)**

Mill departs from Bentham's ideas in one important way: he argues that pleasure can vary in **quality** as well as **quantity**. This means that there are 'lower pleasures' like eating, drinking, sex and playing mindless video games, but also 'higher pleasures' which include friendship, art, reading and conversation. Mill argues that, if we are interested in ensuring our **long-term** happiness, we will focus on the higher pleasures not the lower pleasures.

Mill foresees some criticisms of Utilitarianism and argues against them. Critics complain that it is impossible to calculate all the possible outcomes of every action (*c.f.* **Act Utilitarianism**, p16). Mill's reply is that this isn't necessary. Long experience has taught us that moral rules ("*secondary principles*") like truth-telling, promise-keeping and fair-dealing tend to have happy outcomes, so we can follow these principles most of the time. The Principle of Utility only has to be used when these secondary principles conflict or lead to confusion. This means a utilitarian generally follows the rule of 'keep your promises' but, if she finds she has made a promise to protect a notorious murderer, she can consult the Principle of Utility, which might tell her to break her promise on this occasion.

In ***On Liberty* (1859)**, Mill applies Utilitarianism to politics as the HARM PRINCIPLE:

> *The only purpose for which power can be rightfully exercised over any member of a civilized community, against his will, is to prevent harm to others* – **J.S. Mill**

This is the idea that people should be left free to live as they please so long as they are not harming anyone else by their actions. The Harm Principle has been hugely influential in the 20th and 21st century, supporting the legislation of divorce and homosexuality as well as the decriminalisation of drugs on the grounds that these activities do not cause harm to others.

John A. Robinson

Topic: 2.2 Situation Ethics

J.A.T. Robinson (1919-1983) was a liberal Christian theologian who became the Bishop of Woolwich. His book **Honest To God (1963)** promotes a view of Christian ethics similar to **Joseph Fletcher**'s **Situation Ethics** (p31). Robinson draws on the work of **Paul Tillich** (who also argues for the Law of Love) and **Rudolph Bultmann** (who argues for *"demythologizing"* Christianity by focusing on ethics rather than miracles).

Robinson argues that a new approach to ethics is needed for *"man come of age"*. 'Coming of age' means becoming a mature and responsible adult. Robinson thinks that the human race has 'grown up' in the 20th century: it is no longer superstitious and barbaric, it is scientific and rational, it is largely democratic and supports peace and freedom rather than endless wars. Deontological rules were necessary when the human race was in its 'childhood' but *man come of age* can make ethical decisions without slavishly following rules or being threatened with punishments in Hell or bribed with rewards in Heaven.

Like Fletcher, Robinson rejects a **legalistic approach** to ethics (pp7, 61) in favour of the **Law of Love** (p33). People should act by doing *"what will best demonstrate love for others"*. Robinson argues that this is the meaning behind Jesus' instruction: *"Love your neighbour as yourself"* (**Matthew 22: 39**).

Robinson interprets Jesus as attacking the legalistic ethics of the Jewish religion – only for Christianity then to adopt a similar legalistic ethics. Robinson argues we should go back to Jesus' original intention, which he thinks is revealed in several passages:

- Jesus announces that: *"The Sabbath was made for man, not man for the Sabbath"* (**Mark 2: 27**) – the Sabbath is a Jewish holiday where strict laws forbid any sort of work, but Jesus insists Sabbath laws can be broken in order to do loving work, like helping others
- Jesus breaks religious rules and customs, such as healing people with leprosy (who were considered 'unclean'), talking with solitary women and preaching to Samaritans (non-Jews who were considered enemies at the time)
- In the *pericope adulterae* (p36), Jesus saves a woman from being executed by stoning, saying: *"Let any one of you who is without sin be the first to throw a stone at her"* (**John 8: 7**) – Robinson interprets this as Jesus putting compassion before following rules to the letter

Most traditional Christians reject Robinson's book, pointing out that, although Jesus occasionally breaks religious rules, he also supports them on many occasions. For example, Jesus says *"Do not think that I have come to abolish the Law or the Prophets; I have not come to abolish them but to fulfill them"* (**Matthew 5: 17**).

Critics also point out that the central Christian idea of Christ dying to atone for the sins of mankind makes little sense if morality is **relative** (p7) and there is no fixed framework of right or wrong.

GLOSSARY OF TERMS

Abolition: the banning of slavery

Absolutism: not allowing any exceptions to an ethical code

Act Utilitarianism: type of **Utilitarianism** that proposes **utility** should be calculated to determine the ethical quality of each and every action

Agapeic Ethics: ethics based on following the **Law of Love** rather than ethical rules

Agápē: Greek word for selfless love; basis for **Situation Ethics** and the **Law of Love**

Antinomianism: the rejection of laws, especially ethical laws

Aretē: Greek word for a virtuous personality

Benevolent World Exploder: moral problem for **Utilitarianism** where someone wipes out all life but is considered good because this removes all suffering

Benign Dictator: moral problem for **Utilitarianism** where a ruler takes away people's freedoms but is considered good because he makes people happy

Casuistry: resolving moral problems by applying rules

Civil Rights Movement: a series of campaigns in the 1950s-70s to secure more equality for racial groups, women and people with disabilities

Consequentialism: locating the quality of an ethical act in its consequences

Deontology: duty-based ethics; ethics viewed as laws that must not be broken

Divine Law: portion of the **Eternal Law** that is revealed by God through sacred texts (e.g. the Ten Commandments)

Double Effect: a rule used in **casuistry** that makes it ethically acceptable to do things that break the **Secondary Precepts** of **Natural Moral Law**

Eternal Law: the highest form of goodness as it exists in the mind of God

Eudaimonia: Greek word for happiness; human flourishing in a just society

Eudaimonic ethics: ethics based on promoting a happy society

Evangelical: traditional Christian belief in the Bible being literally true and ethical rules being **absolutist** and strict

Experience Requirement: feature of **Utilitarianism** that requires consequences to be experienced by somebody before they have ay ethical value

Exterior Acts: actions that you carry out but perhaps did not intend

French Revolution: conflict between 1787-1799 when revolutionaries executed the aristocrats in order to promote **human rights**

Harm Principle: liberal principle based on **Utilitarianism** which states that the only basis for restricting a person's behaviour is if it harms someone without their consent

Hedonic Calculus: calculation performed by **Utilitarians** to weigh up the amount of happiness gained or lost by an action or rule

Hedonism: defining good in terms of the amount of pleasure it creates

Human Rights: a set of qualities or behaviours that make up an ethical life; qualities that it can never be ethically right to deprive people

Ideal Utilitarianism: type of **Utilitarianism** that proposes **utility** should be defined as promoting friendship, aesthetic enjoyment and the acquisition of knowledge

Instrumental value: when something is good because of the consequences that come out of it, not for what it is in itself

Interior Acts: actions that you intend to carry out

Intrinsic value: when something is good simply for being what it is not for the consequences that come from it

Karma: concept in Eastern religions that misfortune is due to previous behaviour (perhaps in a previous life)

Law of Love: the principle that selfless love (**agápē**) should be the basis of ethical decisions

Legalism: keeping laws precisely but ignoring the principles behind them

Liberal: rejecting tradition and custom in favour of freedom for the individual; in religious terms, often the opposite of **evangelical**

Methodist: Christian group that was very influential in the **abolition** of slavery

Natural Law: portion of the **Eternal Law** that is revealed in the natural world and in human nature

Natural Moral Law: the **deontological** ethical code that combines **Natural Law** and **Divine Law**

Negative Utilitarianism: type of **Utilitarianism** that proposes **utility** should be defined as avoiding bad consequences (pain, dissatisfaction) rather than bringing about good consequences

New Morality: ethical code that emerged in the mid-20th century, especially the 1960s, promoting personal choice, self expression and a rejection of conventional rules; also a 1966 book by Joseph Fletcher

Objectivism: ethical statements are viewed as facts that apply to everyone equally; the opposite of **relativism**

Ontic Evil: evil that comes about because of the (Fallen) nature of the world, which means that well-intentioned actions still lead to bad consequences

Pericope Adulterae: passage in John 7:52-8:12 in which Jesus defends a woman caught in the act of adultery

Permissive Society: term for the culture of the 1960s that promoted the **New Morality** and relaxed ethical rules on sexual behaviour, self expression, drug taking and family values

Positive Law: the law of the land or customs that people follow; often imperfectly based on **Natural Law** or **Divine Law**

Primary Precepts: guiding principles of **Natural Moral Law**, including preserving life, reproduction, education, worshiping God and living in an orderly society

Preference Utilitarianism: version of **Utilitarianism** that proposes **utility** should be defined as the satisfying of wants or preferences

Proportionalism: a deontological ethical theory based on **Natural Moral Law** that allows the **Secondary Precepts** to be broken when it leads to proportionally more good than bad consequences

Psychological Egoism: the idea that pleasure is the only thing that motivates people to do anything

Relativism: viewing all ethical codes as relative or matters of personal choice; the opposite of **objectivism**

Right Act: an action which, according to **Proportionalism**, is ethically acceptable because it has the right intentions

Rule Utilitarianism: type of **Utilitarianism** that proposes **utility** should be calculated to determine the ethical quality of following a rule

Secondary Precepts: specific rules in **Natural Moral Law** that are worked out from the **Primary Precepts**

Situation Ethics: an ethical system that locates the ethical quality of an act in its loving motivation

Teleological ethics: ethics based on achieving the goal or end of human life (this includes both **Natural Moral Law** and **Utilitarianism**)

Telos: Greek word for the goal, end or purpose of life

Totalitarian: a regime that rejects individual freedoms and attempts to dictate what good and evil mean in terms of their value to the state

Trolley Problem: ethical problem proposed by Philippa Foot involving the choice between killing a single person or allowing a group of people to die

Utilitarianism: a **consequentialist** ethical system that focuses on the **utility** of actions as the basis of ethical judgments

Utility: the desirable outcome for **Utilitarianism**; may be pleasure, happiness, satisfied preferences or other things

TOPIC 2 IN THE EXAM

AS-Level Paper 2 (Religion & Ethics)

Section A

1   Explore the key ideas of *agape* as a basis for ethical decision making. (8 marks)

"Explore" questions award marks for AO1 (knowledge & understanding). You don't need to evaluate these ideas – just describe them. This question is pretty broad but it could be phrased more specifically, such as "explore the key ideas about Utilitarianism".

2   Assess the significance of changes in social attitudes for **either** Situation Ethics **or** Natural Moral Law. (9 marks)

"Assess the value" questions award some marks for AO1 (3 marks in this question) but more for AO2 (evaluation – 6 marks in this question). You need to describe a bit about the content of this topic (with reference to an ethical theory), but also the debates concerning how they have encouraged or or been opposed by changes in social attitudes.

3   Assess the strengths of proportionalism as an ethical theory. (9 marks)

"Assess the strengths" questions award some marks for AO1 (3 marks in this question) but more for AO2 (evaluation – 6 marks in this question). You need to describe a bit about the content of this topic (such as Bernard Hoose's views), but more about the debates concerning how it improves on Natural Moral Law.

Section B

4   (a) Explore the role of pleasure in ethical decision making. (8 marks)

Another "explore" question that only awards marks for AO1 (knowledge & understanding), so all that is required is description. If you only describe one role (such as Bentham's hedonic calculus), then you cannot attain higher than Level 2 (5/8).

(b) Analyse the view that religious approaches are not compatible with Utilitarianism. (20 marks)

This "Analyse" question awards some marks for AO1 (5 marks in this question), but mostly for AO2 (15 marks in this question). You need to describe a bit about the content (such as what Utilitarianism is), but more about whether or not it is compatible with religious ethics (such as the Ten Commandments or Natural Moral Law)

Total = 54 marks

A-Level Paper 2 (Religion & Ethics)

Section A

1   Explore the role of absolutism in ethical decision making. (8 marks)

"Explore" questions award marks for AO1 (knowledge & understanding). You don't need to evaluate these ideas – just describe them. This question is pretty specific but it could be phrased more broadly, such as "explore Natural Moral Law".

2   Assess the view that Natural Moral Law remains appropriate for ethical decision making. (12 marks)

"Assess" questions award some marks for AO1 (4 marks in this question) but more for AO2 (evaluation – 8 marks in this question). You need to describe a bit about the content of this topic (such as the Primary and Secondary Precepts), but also the debates concerning how they should be applied (e.g. in civil rights, gender relations and in reforming the law).

Section B

Read the following passage before answering the questions.

> If all men were saints, then situation ethics would be the perfect ethics. John A. T. Robinson has called situation ethics 'the only ethic for man come of age'. This is probably true – but man has not yet come of age. Man, therefore, still needs the crutch and the protection of law. If we insist that in every situation every man must make his own decision, then first of all we must make man morally and lovingly fit to take that decision; otherwise we need the compulsion of law to make him do it. And the fact is that few of us have reached that stage; we still need law, we still need to be told what to do, and sometimes even to be compelled to do it.
>
> … the situationist points out again and again that in his view there is nothing which is intrinsic ally good or bad. Goodness and badness, as he puts it, are not properties, they are predicates. They are not inbuilt qualities; they happen to a thing in a given situation. I am very doubtful if the distinction between goodness and badness can be so disposed of.
>
> **Taken from**: *Ethic s in a Permissive Society, by William Barclay (Collins1971) Chapter 4, Situation Ethic s, pp.69–91.*

3   (a) Clarify the ideas illustrated in this passage about the weaknesses of Situation Ethics. *You must refer to the passage in your response.* (10 marks)

"Clarify" questions only award marks for AO1 (knowledge & understanding), so all that is required is description. There is no need to evaluate whether the strengths of Situationalism outweigh the weaknesses – just explain Barclay's criticism in this passage and the Anthology extract as a whole.

(b) Analyse the claim that the 'New Morality' of the 20th century has helped with ethical decision-making. **(20 marks)**

This "Analyse" question awards some marks for AO1 (5 marks in this question), but mostly for AO2 (15 marks in this question). You need to describe a bit about the content (such as what agape means), but more about whether or not this approach helps us solve ethical problems.

Section C

4   "Ethical problems can be resolved by asking yourself, What would Jesus do?"

Evaluate this view in the context ethics. In your response to this question, you must include how environmental ethics links to one of the following:

- Philosophy of Religion
- New Testament Studies
- The Study of a Religion

(30 marks)

This "Evaluate" question awards some marks for AO1 (5 marks in this question), but mostly for AO2 (25 marks in this question). You need to describe a bit about the content (such as the ministry of Jesus), but more about whether this is a helpful insight for ethical decision making in the 21st century In order to attain beyond the top of level 4 (i.e. score 25+) you must link to another area of the course (such as the Existence of God or the Problem of Evil, Jesus' ethical teachings or the key moral principles of Christianity).

Total = 90 marks

In these examples, all the questions are drawn from Topic 2. A real AS exam would draw from Topics 1-3 and a real A-Level exam would draw from Topics 4-6 as well.

LOOKING AHEAD...

So far, you have been introduced to four main ethical theories. In this Topic, you have studied Utilitarianism, Situation Ethics and Natural Moral Law and, in Topic 1, you were introduced to Kantian ethics (which A-Level students will explore in more detail in Year 2). You will next have the opportunity to apply these theories to two particularly fraught areas of human experience: war and sex.

The Ethics of War & Peace

It's common to hear talk as if war is simply the worst of all human activities, something which can never be ethical or just. However, further thought raises some questions about this.

Utilitarianism demands that we maximize utility (pleasure or satisfaction, usually) and it's not hard to think of scenarios where this could be done more effectively through war than through peace. For example, a swift attack on a country that was carrying out atrocities or threatening its neighbours.

Similarly, **Natural Moral Law** proposes that we should live together in an orderly society and this seems to justify using war against neighbours who threaten that orderly society. Even **Situation Ethics** seems to accept that acts of war can be the most loving thing to do in a particular set of circumstances.

Set against these views is the insistence of PACIFICISM that war is always the greatest of evils and a course of action that can never be justified.

Sexual Ethics

Traditional ethics have looked on sex as a very dangerous and troubling form of human experience. Sexual motives often come from our irrational natures and many ethicists (such as utilitarians and NML) argue that ethics ought to be a matter of rational choice. Sex unleashes powerful forces of possessiveness, jealousy, anger, shame and loss. It also leads to particularly serious consequences: pregnancy, disease and the formation (or breakup) of lifelong relationships.

The liberal ethics of the New Morality views sex more positively, as an act of love, as a source of recreational fun, even as a type of self-expression (and therefore a human right). The old distinction between selfless love (*agápē*) and the other, lesser types of love has become blurred. Sexual love is viewed by some people as just as innocent, even as noble, as charity and compassion.

Against this background, Situation Ethics tries to assert the old distinction between *agápē* and other types of love – but the distinction is often missed by people who justify divorce or casual sex as acting out of 'love'. Natural Moral Law still urges humans to live rationally and restrict sex to married heterosexual couples raising children. Utilitarianism, with its commitment to maximising happiness, sometimes seems to endorse any and all types of sexual behaviour, so long as everyone involved consents.

ABOUT THE AUTHOR

Jonathan Rowe is a teacher of Religious Studies, Psychology and Sociology at Spalding Grammar School and he creates and maintains **www.philosophydungeon.weebly.com** and the **www.psychologywizard.net** site for Edexcel A-Level Psychology. He has worked as an examiner for various Exam Boards but is not affiliated with Edexcel. This series of books grew out of the resources he created for his students. Jonathan also writes novels and creates resources for his hobby of fantasy wargaming. He likes warm beer and smooth jazz.

Printed in Great Britain
by Amazon

34808732R00052